GET REAL

*The courage to be wrong
and
the power to change*

GET REAL

*The courage to be wrong
and
the power to change*

CARMEL WYNNE

MERCIER PRESS

Dedication

To my daughters, Deirdre Anne Wynne Robinson and Aoife Marie Mockler and my friend, Liz Harper. Thanks for your loving support and help.

MERCIER PRESS
Cork
www.mercierpress.ie

© Carmel Wynne, 2025

ISBN: 978-1-917453-20-2

978-1-917453-21-9 eBook

This book is sold subject to the condition that it shall not, by way of trade or otherwise, be lent, resold, hired out or otherwise circulated without the publisher's prior consent in any form of binding or cover other than that in which it is published and without a similar condition including this condition being imposed on the subsequent purchaser.

No part of this publication may be reproduced or transmitted in any form or by any means, electronic or mechanical, including photocopying, recording or any information or retrieval system, without the prior permission of the publisher in writing.

Printed and bound in the EU.

Contents

Author's Note	6
The Quest for Happiness	7
Emotional Pain is a Wake-up Call	23
Take Responsibility for Your own Happiness	34
Continued Influence Effect	49
Is it You or Your Programming?	62
The Masks we Wear and the Roles we Play	74
Home Truths	89
You are Not your Thoughts	104
Defence Mechanisms	115
Holding Yourself Accountable with a Light Touch	131
Dealing with Internal Conflict	144
Communication is Complex	158
Reframing Beliefs	173
Know Yourself	189
Spirituality	204
Epilogue	219
Bibliography	221

Author's Note

Throughout this book, names have been given to fictional individuals that are based on real scenarios I have encountered in my twenty-three years of practice as a life coach. These are anecdotal stories that illustrate typical real-life conflicts people may experience and suggest ways to resolve them. None of these stories relates explicitly to real-life cases.

Carmel Wynne

1

THE QUEST FOR HAPPINESS

One of the most tragic things I know about human nature is that all of us tend to put off living. We are all dreaming of some magical rose garden over the horizon instead of enjoying the roses that are blooming outside our windows today.

DALE CARNEGIE

Tales of quests figure prominently in the folklore of every country. Put simply, a quest is an odyssey in pursuit of something of great value. The hero, usually a male in these narratives, sets out on an arduous journey in search of something precious. On his adventure, he faces challenges and trials, and early in the story, he meets a wise mentor.

Heroes are not always brave. Some initially refuse to go on the quest. When circumstances force them to set out, they conquer their fears. As they journey on, each hero becomes braver, more determined, and more resourceful. At the end of the expedition, when the hero finds what he was looking for, he has overcome great difficulties, is transformed, and an inspiration to others.

The *Oxford Dictionary* definition of quest is 'a long search for something, especially for some quality such as happiness'. You don't have to believe me when I tell you that any person who enters into a marriage or who agrees to be in a committed, monogamous, enduring partnership is on a quest, whether they are aware of this or not.

Some of the most intense feelings a person can experience

are generated by falling in love. Most people would agree that this can be a thrilling, exciting, passionate and intoxicating experience. However, making a life-changing decision while in the throes of the 'in love stage' poses a significant risk. It's highly likely that your personal experiences of falling in and out of love have made you aware that the euphoric feelings don't last. If time has not mercifully dimmed your memory, you may recall your first experiences of being in love. Adolescent romances are usually over in a matter of weeks. In retrospect, you may recall how happy your adolescent self felt, but it may be hard to remember what made you fall in love in the first place.

A wise person would never suggest to someone who is deeply in love that their feelings will change and will continue to change if a partnership lasts. Two people who are caught up in the sheer pleasure of being in love cannot judge whether what they feel is the real thing or only a physical attraction. It would be foolish to underestimate the power of instant attraction. For some, it hits like a thunderbolt, which strikes across a crowded room. Two people make eye contact. The connection is electric and the emotional impact is real and feels magical.

Mutual attraction happens instantly. The emotional response is so strong and all-consuming that it may seem that fate has intervened. Emotions start as sensations in the body, and feelings are generated from our thoughts about those emotions. When you are in love, you are completely besotted with the other person. Sexual attraction is such an essential element in a love relationship that early on, it is hard to tell if lust is masquerading as love.

During the initial romantic stage, the willingness of each person to put their partner first, the openness to see things from the other's viewpoint, even when they do not agree, and the desire to spend every waking moment together is intoxicating. Assuming that a highly romantic state is 'true love' can lead to an unhealthy partnership.

I have coached people who knew on a practical level that their partner was wrong for them but the attraction was so strong that they allowed the heart to rule the head. There is no denying that the highly charged in-love state leads to distorted perceptions. If intimate partner violence occurs once, there is a probability that it will occur again. The tragedy is that I've met people who knew this and went on to marry the perpetrator.

While you see your partner through rose-tinted spectacles it is easy to be blind to the ordinary parts of your partner's character that may disappoint, frustrate or disturb you when reality clicks in.

The problem with emotions is it is hard to be objective about them and impossible to explain or understand them well. The fantasy world of lovers has an expiry date. Can you guess why romantic novels end when the couple are madly and passionately in love? The quest for love is a universal theme in romantic fiction. Readers of this genre, who are mostly women, desire emotionally satisfying, happy endings.

The central love story in romantic fiction is a quest. The story involves many twists, turns and adventures that involve bravery and robust values until finally the main characters realise they are in love. When in the final chapter the handsome hero says something like, 'Marry me, and I will make you happy'; the beautiful woman is overjoyed and says, 'Yes'. What is left unsaid but implied is, 'They lived happily ever after'.

When a couple are madly in love, problems don't seem to matter, but eventually something will happen to end the fantasy.

Occasionally, what should be a happy event, such as marrying or becoming parents, will break the spell. Disillusionment will set in, the rose-tinted spectacles will come off and the character flaws, defects and imperfections that the partner was blind to previously will become an issue.

If this happens, some couples find they are in trouble. The development of a partnership involves many factors. Falling in love does not mean that a couple is compatible. It would be wonderful if there were a formula or checklist that would predict an enduring partnership. The truth is no one can accurately predict the future.

As the intense in-love feelings fade away, similarities and differences emerge which were not thought about before partners took the big step of moving in together. The wake-up call for some is the realisation that they really don't know each other. It comes as a shock when couples discover that they have different values, interests, goals and radically different views on what is a fair division of finances, household chores and visits with their extended families.

Of course, partners have long conversations before they get married or agree to be in a committed, monogamous relationship. Some partners talk about their attitudes, values and expectations, but many don't because they never had to think about or define them.

A lot of our most basic views on how intimate partners should treat each other are based on what was modelled for us by our parents. When I coach clients who have communication difficulties in either their personal or professional lives, I introduce them to the concept of breaking the 'psychological contract'.

The concept of the psychological contract emerged in the early 1960s. It refers to an unwritten set of beliefs, values, perceptions and ambitions employers and employees have of each other. As the expectations and assumptions are not directly communicated or verbalised, it is covert, imprecise and implicit. In other words, the expectations are hinted at but never directly expressed.

Alex and Jamie were a volatile couple who loved each other, but they fought almost every day. Rows over silly things were a constant feature of their relationship. An hour after a fight, neither could say what exactly they fought over, but the tension between them persisted until they made up, and hurt their relationship.

An avid reader of self-help books, Jamie believed that conversations about issues and sharing their feelings should bring them closer. They talked a lot, but talking did not bring them closer. Often it made things worse rather than better.

When talking about problems only exacerbates the situation, it's highly probable that the unspoken expectations and assumptions couples have of each other are the cause. Misunderstandings, hurt feelings and an erosion of trust are inevitable when expectations are not directly communicated and verbalised.

Jamie admitted that when she felt stressed and worried about their financial situation, it put both of them on edge and they were likely to quarrel. Jamie was sensitive to Alex's moods and tried not to do anything to cause annoyance if Alex was on edge. She was aware that when either of them was stressed, anything could start a row. It might be a letter from the bank advising that an account was overdrawn, a forgotten errand or a disagreement about household chores.

Jamie's perception was she was always quick to offer a sincere and heartfelt apology. Alex had a very different view, claiming that Jamie rarely said 'sorry'. Alex found it hard to stay patient when Jamie was to do something, then forgot and made light of the omission.

Jamie felt hurt that Alex never appreciated the effort she put into looking nice for him or creating a romantic setting when she prepared a special meal. It hurt that he rarely gave her the 'thank you' or expressions of gratitude she expected for the work she put into special occasions.

The lockdown during the global pandemic had unexpected and unforeseen consequences that neither of them could have predicted. Their disagreements had started to escalate into angry rows. It was understandable that being cooped up in a small, one-bedroom apartment, tempers flared. It scared Jamie that she was beginning to feel bitterness and a dislike of Alex.

When they married, the couple made an agreement that they would never let the sun set on a disagreement without making up. The night that Jamie stormed off to bed in silence without saying 'good night' was a wake-up call for both of them.

Before lockdown, when Alex was angry, he walked away. He was upset when Jamie did the same and went to bed without making up. He wished he trusted her to keep their agreements.

Alex loved Jamie passionately. He liked that they could talk freely and openly much of the time, that they shared the same values, and he anticipated Jamie would understand how she hurt his feelings. The breaking of an agreement was a breach of trust, something he would never have expected from her.

As Alex brooded on what was happening with his partner, he had an insight that shocked him. Most of their fights were about the breaking of trust when agreements that had never been verbalised were broken. His assumption was that because Jamie loved him, she should be aware of his expectations and live up to them. The betrayal he felt at the perceived breaking of agreements was frustrating and hurtful for him, but unfair to Jamie.

Beautiful and positive changes happened when Alex shared his shattering revelation with his wife. Jamie, who was not as self-aware as Alex, admitted that alone in her bed, she felt hurt, angry and betrayed. She felt concerned when Alex broke his promise and he didn't follow her in to say 'good night'.

Jamie was astonished that Alex was not turning out to be the perfect husband she wanted him to be. In many ways, Alex was a wonderful man; funny, kind, generous to a fault, but Jamie never expected that he would take her for granted or forget to say 'thank you'.

The strong feelings of love and happiness that are there during the initial wonderful stages of a partnership lessen and are weakened when daily life intrudes and partners do not live up to each other's expectations. This process is gradual, unconscious and inevitable.

Within a couple of years, many partners have established a pattern of nagging and fighting about what the other does or doesn't want to do. He says he's going to the pub with his friends, but she complains that he is not spending time with her and their baby. He feels nagged, and she feels frustrated.

As romance declines, each person's willingness to make their partner's needs important lessens. The openness to seeing things from the other's viewpoint changes, and the desire to spend every waking moment together is no longer intoxicating. You don't need experts to tell you that your needs and wants are constantly changing. As partners' needs change, some couples find they engage in less sexual activity. The way we experience, receive and give love changes as our moods, perceptions, beliefs and life circumstances change.

Assumptions that partners who get married want the same things are as illogical as thinking you can read your partner's mind. Partners take a huge gamble if they decide to get married and commit to loving each other 'until death do us part'. Many people do not understand that living together cannot show partners how little they know about their hidden expectations of marriage.

There are many reasons why the frequency of sex diminishes. Some couples never talk about their sexual needs. If partners become disillusioned, disappointed and frustrated with each other, romantic feelings decrease, and they have sex less often. Lack of emotional intimacy can result in the partnership losing its spark and generating deep unhappiness.

I believe that every person who stays married to a spouse or remains in a committed, monogamous, enduring partnership is a hero or a heroine. To promise to love your partner, day after day, week after week, year after year, for the rest of your life is taking a monumental gamble.

On his quest, the hero must overcome fears, develop courage, become resourceful and have the motivation to stay focused on the goal as he pushes forward and remains determined not to give up. To make a lifetime contract, one has to conquer fear. When you feel vulnerable, it takes courage to have an honest conversation, to allow yourself to be vulnerable, to share how you feel and explain why you feel the way you do, and to stay motivated and determined not to give up on your partner.

If there is a more frequently misused word in the English language than 'love', I don't know what it is. When couples come for relationship coaching, I have the integrity to tell them, 'You don't know this yet, but please trust me, I'm confident that you have the solution to your problems. If you allow me to challenge your language, beliefs and assumptions, I will ask you questions that will empower you to work out how to co-operate in resolving your problems.'

There are endless theories about what a couple can do to build a solid, loving and enduring partnership. Only a very privileged few are born to parents who make excellent role models for a great partnership. The best modelling comes from parents who enjoy physical and sexual intimacy, have the ability to communicate honestly, demonstrate the skills to negotiate and manage conflict and empower each child in the family to feel loved and lovable.

Sometimes, the best thing that can happen for people is to question the beliefs and values they hold about love and happiness. Through his work as a marriage counsellor, Dr Gary Chapman developed the concept of the five love languages. These are words of affirmation, acts of service, receiving gifts, quality time and physical touch. When partners learn each other's love languages, it increases their intimacy, sense of connection and feelings of closeness between them.

The qualities that each person being coached will need on their personal quest are like those required of the hero. He can never predict what lies ahead, but whether it be finding the Golden Fleece or overcoming an enemy, he is motivated to succeed. Through hardship and personal struggles, he persists and continues his quest, determined to reach his goal. In the process, he learns to overcome his fears and becomes so brave and resourceful that the adventure transforms him.

I have spent decades observing family relationships, studying research findings, and reading books and articles on love, marriage, separation and divorce. What I have learned from all my reading, my own life experience and the couples I have coached is that regardless of whether we are single, married or in a committed relationship, we are all on a lifelong quest for love and happiness.

Partners who have different love languages give and re- ceive love in different ways. John and Mary were attending a counsellor for marital issues. Part of their homework was to do something nice for each other. When they came back for their next session, the counsellor asked how the homework went. Mary glared at John and said, 'He didn't do it'. John was highly indignant.

He explained that on Saturday, he got up early and went out at 9 o'clock to clean, vacuum and wax the car because Mary liked it to look nice. Unaware of the effort he was making to please her, Mary lay in bed feeling hurt and disappointed. John was up so early that Mary expected him to bring her breakfast in bed. She was disappointed that he didn't. Misunderstandings like this occur very often when partners fail to appreciate their different love languages.

During the following week, Mary felt unhappy, disappointed, and angry with John. He was supposed to do something nice for her, but instead he spent the morning working on the car. During the week, Mary was cold and matter-of-fact. John was aware that she blamed him for something that upset her. The non-verbal communication of her displeasure was evident, but he had no idea why she was unhappy or what he had done to cause her negative reaction.

John's love language was acts of service, which frequently went unnoticed. Mary changed her attitude once she acknowledged John's effort to please her. She was gracious enough to express her appreciation and honest enough to share that he would have received more kudos if he had brought her breakfast in bed.

The revelation for John was that he went through a miserable week, feeling bad for upsetting Mary. Had he told Mary that his plan to do something nice for her was to get up and clean and wax the car, she might have thanked him but said that what she would really love was breakfast in bed. Had he joined her in bed, they could have spent quality time together and he would have spared himself hours of work.

The insight for Mary was how much she took for granted. Appreciating the practical things that John did for her, such as stacking the dishwasher, hanging out the washing because she didn't like clothes dried in the tumble drier and leaving out the bins, was a game-changer. The life lesson they both learned was that your partner cannot know what you don't tell them.

If you ask parents what they want for their children, the majority will say that they want them to be happy. You may well ask, doesn't everyone want to be happy? Of course, the answer is yes, but if you are like most people, you will not have specific criteria for measuring contentment. The American Psychological Association defines happiness as 'an emotion of joy, gladness, satisfaction and wellbeing'. Getting a list of four different words for one emotion is a problem for me when I coach. If I ask a client, 'What do you want?' and the person tells me five different things, I know that client will be difficult to satisfy.

My positive intention in inviting readers to think about setting out on a quest is that the client is the only person who can name the criteria they use to measure love or happiness. No two people experience emotions in the same way. The American philosopher Ralph Waldo Emerson is quoted as saying, 'Life is a journey, not a destination.' Some pundits suggest we never arrive, but on the journey, we become different people because we mature and change.

It's well documented that a relationship is only as good as its communication. How openly and honestly partners communicate determines the quality of intimacy in a partnership. Miscommunication and misunderstandings occur because people have different language skills and attention spans. Some only listen to words, miss non-verbal cues, and fail to hear the whole message.

Say I am coaching a client and we are working on goal-setting. An achievable goal needs to be:

- Stated in positive language
- Measurable
- Achievable
- Realistic
- Timed

At face value, the sentence, 'I want to be happy' appears to meet the criteria for goal-setting. It appears to be a simple sentence until you become aware of the ambiguity of the English language. The complexity of communication becomes clear when we find that words such as 'love' and 'happiness' mean different things to different people and in different contexts.

There is bound to be confusion and misunderstanding when people assume that they have identical meanings for those words and they don't. Can you believe that you and your partner may as well be speaking two different languages if you give different meanings to the same words? It is sometimes necessary to define the meaning of a word if you are seeking clarity and want to avoid confusion and misunderstandings.

You can understand why there is a language issue if a client suggests that feeling joy, gladness, satisfaction and wellbeing is a measure of happiness. A definition I like is, 'Happiness is a word used to describe a feeling. This emotion is unique to the person who is in the state of being happy.' A useful definition of 'emotion' is, 'a strong feeling deriving from one's circumstances, mood or relationships with others'.

To find a shared meaning for words such as 'happiness' and 'love' illustrates the complexity of communication. I have explained how problems occur because of the ambiguity of words and how partners who have different love languages may have issues with incompatibility.

You understand every word in the sentence, 'I want to be happy'. Happiness is a concept which I'm going to define as a thought or feeling about a desire to feel a certain way. I would prefer not to engage in semantics, but for the purposes of clarity, it's necessary. The person on a quest for love and happiness wants to feel a certain way and we simply don't have the language that is adequate to describe how that experience feels.

Say I hand you a sprig of the herb lavender. You can see it, touch it, taste it and smell it. Yet if I ask you to describe what lavender smells like, it cannot be done. You could say it's like this or that but those comparisons only offer clues as to what you experience.

Whether a person has a positive response or a negative reaction to something they taste will depend on their personal preference. Broccoli is one of those vegetables that people either love or hate. If you ask me, 'What does broccoli taste like?' I will say, 'It's delicious'. My friend who hates all green vegetables might say, 'It tastes disgusting and it smells bad'.

If you cannot accurately describe the smell or taste of the herb that you hold in your hand, is there any wonder that when you attempt to talk about feelings, there is a lot of mind-reading and guesswork involved? An important step for people whose desired outcome is to resolve the conflict issues that occur in their relationship is to understand how difficult it is to communicate with clarity.

Once partners understand that words are inadequate to describe an experience, it's helpful for them to learn how to listen in order to hear the intended meaning. This may sound as if I'm excessively concerned with minor details, but please bear with me. What makes person-to-person communication complicated is that a person can hear and understand the words' meaning but fails to notice what is implied by tone of voice, eye contact, body language and what is hinted at and not verbalised.

Words such as 'love' and 'happiness' mean what a person assumes they mean. It's challenging to develop an awareness of how words and concepts fragment reality. A concept is static, while reality is constantly changing. A common expression relating to adaptable partners is, 'they go with the flow'. The term 'in flow', as originally coined, has nothing to do with water. It describes feeling immersed and engaged in an activity.

Communication would be easier if there were just one definition for a word. Take the word 'river' for example. From the *Oxford Advanced Learner's Dictionary*, I learned that a 'river' is a large amount of liquid that is flowing in a particular direction. Rivers of molten lava flowed down the mountain. Google gave me, 'A river is a ribbon-like body of water that flows downhill from the force of gravity. A river can be wide and deep or shallow enough for a person to wade across. A flowing body of water that is smaller than a river is called a stream, creek or brook'.

Say I have a blind friend who has never seen a river. She asks me to describe turbulent water in a rapidly flowing river so she can get a feel for what the flow of fast water is like. So,

I dip a bucket into the water to bring it to her, but it can't be done. Once the water stops flowing, all I bring her is liquid in a bucket.

Like the ebb and flow of the tides, people go through emotional cycles of positive and negative emotions, such as joy and sadness, happiness and unhappiness, engagement and disengagement. Has anyone ever told you that partners in enduring relationships drop out of love and may have to put in a lot of effort to fall back in love again? The sadness every time a partner falls out of love is painful, and for a time, it can feel like one's heart is breaking.

The problems that arise in every partnership test the strength of each partner's commitment to the partnership. The more deeply in love a person is with a partner, the more deeply they feel the pain when they drop out of love. Some partners make the decision to separate the first time cracks appear in the partnership. Others who are in it for the long haul try to work through their problems and rekindle their love. Others still stay together when there is no love, and they lead separate lives as partners in name only.

I doubt if there is a person in any enduring partnership who has not suffered the deep emotional pain of feeling so distressed that it appears as if your heart has cracked inside your chest. When one's emotional heart is breaking, there are no shortcuts to fast forward through the sadness, pain and grief. However, broken hearts can be mended and partnerships can be strengthened and healed.

The romantic phase of my marriage ended three days before our second wedding anniversary when the first of our four daughters was born. Caring for a baby changed my husband Colm's and my priorities. Identifying as parents altered our lives and forced a long series of adjustments. There is little time for romance when caring for a newborn, breast-fed baby who disrupts sleep.

I gave up work to be a full-time mother. By comparison, my husband's life didn't change much as he went back to his job and was able to continue with his hobbies. You could say that we had a different kind of marriage in our parenting phase. I will admit that a period of disillusionment set in for me as my life went through a huge upheaval in the second, parenting phase of my marriage.

The third phase started when our youngest was a teenager and I went back to work. With that newfound freedom, Colm and I set out to be SKI parents – spending our kid's inheritance as we frequently holidayed abroad.

Recently, I shocked a friend when I said I was married three times, then added, 'to the same man'. Each phase of my marriage changed who I was and how I related. The passion and excitement I enjoyed when I first fell in love could never be recreated, but each time I fell back in love with my husband, we had a better-quality marriage.

2

EMOTIONAL PAIN IS A WAKE-UP CALL

If you are depressed, you are living in the past. If you are anxious, you are living in the future.

LAO TZU

Before you can experience a happy, joyful, fulfilled life with a partner, it's essential for you to feel happy, fulfilled and joyful in yourself. Emotional pain is a wake-up call, which you would do well to look on as an invitation to reflect on the quality of the life you are living. Emotions such as hurt, anger, disappointment, resentment or dissatisfaction are the body's stress response to perceived negative interactions or events.

When people feel stressed, the body releases adrenaline and cortisol, the fight or flight hormones that give an instant energy boost. In a stressful situation, many of us veer towards flight rather than fight. The inclination is to run and avoid uncomfortable situations, if possible. People have a true emotional response to what they believe to be real and in many situations what people assume to be a threat is not necessarily a real threat.

When you encounter a perceived threat, your hypothalamus, a tiny region at your brain's base, sets off an alarm system in your body. This prompts your adrenal glands to release a surge of hormones, including adrenaline and cortisol. Once the perceived threat has passed, hormone levels return to normal. The adrenaline and cortisol levels drop, and the heart rate and blood pressure return to normal.

When the brain experiences pain over and over, neural pathways get strengthened and sensitised. Neuroplastic pain is driven by fear and avoidance. When we fear and avoid pain, we reinforce the signals that we are threatened and in danger. This reinforced fear of pain leads to avoidance and the fear and avoidance lead to more pain, and it becomes a vicious cycle.

Chronic stress takes a huge toll on the body and wreaks havoc on both the mind and body. Your body's natural alarm system also communicates with the brain regions that control mood, motivation and fear. The body's stress response system is usually self-limiting but if stressors are always present and a person feels under constant attack, the fight-or-flight reaction stays turned on. Over-exposure to cortisol and other stress hormones puts you at increased risk of many health problems.

People who suffered from neglect or were abused as children are particularly vulnerable to stress and anxiety. Traumatic events that can be traced back to childhood are often responsible for strong stress reactions. No two people react to stress in the same way. Some people seem calm and relaxed about almost everything. Others have a strong reaction to what appear to be minor stresses and others still have such an over-the-top reaction that even a broken fingernail invites a drama.

Negative thinking produces stress hormones that are addictive. Just as people can be addicted to alcohol or cocaine, a person can be addicted to stress and, like a drug addict, need a bigger fix all the time. Stress management specialist Debbie Mandel, the author of *Addicted to Stress*, suggested that 'Obsessing over work allows people to avoid self-reflection and run away from their own unhappiness'.

'Psychogenic pain' is the term for pain that is primarily caused by psychological factors, such as depression and anxiety.

It feels the same as pain from a physical injury or illness because it involves the same brain processes, and in cases of chronic pain, the brain helps perpetuate it. If you feel depressed, anxious, undermined, frustrated, angry or dissatisfied, the emotional pain you experience is as real as if you were dealing with a broken leg.

The medical profession has had great success in treating acute pain caused by bone fractures. Broken bones heal in a matter of weeks when the correct diagnosis is made, the injury is treated and the patient is compliant and faithful to their schedule of physiotherapy exercises. The chronic pain that comes from being broken-hearted doesn't show up on an X-ray or MRI scan. In a busy medical practice, doctors tend to treat the symptoms that the patient names during the consultation. Even when physicians are aware of family problems that contribute to a patient's emotional suffering, they are not trained to deal with emotional issues that generate chronic stress.

The body experiences what you and I might think of as normal everyday stress as a threat. When people feel insecure, anxious and worried, their bodies feel as if they are constantly under attack. Hard-wired to deal with danger with the fight-or-flight response, we are not set up to tolerate the high levels of unremitting stress of chronic emotional pain, which people experience when they are in turmoil, feel unsafe, undermined and dissatisfied.

Our thoughts generate our emotions, and most of us are not good at getting in touch with what we are thinking. Often, we are working on auto-pilot and don't challenge the negative thinking that fuels feelings of dissatisfaction, unhappiness, depression, anxiety, disappointment or the sense that we are stuck in a rut.

Living with negative feelings is stressful and takes a toll

on our bodies. Stress is a fact of daily life in our world today. Whether you are aware of this or not, you always have choices about how you deal with stress. In every situation, when you choose to do one thing, you unconsciously make choices not to do a whole lot of other things. For example, when I decided to sit at the computer to write today, I chose to ignore my emails and not go for a walk, weed the garden, or telephone a friend.

You have beliefs about what you need, want and cannot do without. Stress is generated when your needs are not met. When you feel dissatisfied, a part of you wants something you're not getting. You could think of the emotional distress you experience when your needs are not met as an alarm signal that is warning you of a pending problem. Emotional distress that you ignore will not disappear. Over time, it can build up and grow and, given the right conditions, will ignite. For example, Pam was annoyed at having to remind her teenage son to empty the dishwasher constantly. She realised how her annoyance had built up and grown out of control the night she screamed at her son in an explosive outburst of rage.

Every person has the capacity to act naturally and spontaneously, but very few have the freedom to do so. You are one hundred per cent responsible for every thought you decide to focus on. When a thought pops into your head, you always have a choice. You can hold onto the thought and engage with the emotional response you get. If you are not happy with the response, you can simply change the thought.

If you decide to think about how badly your partner acted last week or six months or five years ago, you are choosing to marinade in toxic feelings. Your mood contributes to how memories are recalled. Your memories and perceptions change when your mood changes. Your sense of self, who you were in any event you recollect, is unstable, but remember that facts do not change.

Your memories do not exist outside of you. When you go to the cinema and watch a film, you are drawn into the drama. You react to what is on the screen even though you are aware that you are watching actors projected onto a screen. Your emotions are triggered by what appears real until the film ends. Your memories are fantasies that are ephemeral, unless you replay them and refuse to let them go.

Once you believe that the present moment is never intolerable and you learn to live life one moment at a time, you can live a stress-free life. Does this sound like a wonderful theory but impossible to put into practice? Staying calm and relaxed in stressful situations takes effort, practice, and, most of all, changes in what you believe you can and can't control.

Current research on brain neuroplasticity has alerted many physicians to the science underlying neuroplastic and psychogenic pain. As researchers gain a deeper understanding of how interconnected the body, mind and spirit are, doctors who strive to get to the root cause of a patient's pain are confirming what philosophers and non-medical practitioners have understood for centuries: The pain in the heart of a person who feels heartbroken is genuine pain.

Every thought we think generates a response in the body. The brain plays a major role in whether the reaction is pleasant or painful. A person's expectations and beliefs influence the processing of pain signals and can tune them up or down. Research in medicine, neuroscience and psychology supports the belief that chronic physical pain can be exacerbated and, in some cases, generated by neural pathways in the brain.

How people feel pain is influenced by their genetic make-up, emotions, personality, past experiences and lifestyle. People who fall into the trap of catastrophising thoughts and have negative expectations amplify their pain. Scientists Luana Colloca and Beth Daniels suggest that catastrophising thinking is like picking up a can of petrol and pouring it on a fire.

The severity of migraines and the symptoms from chronic joint and muscle pain is affected by how people think about their own pain. In a study conducted in Australia's University of New South Wales, students believed they were signing up for an anti-anxiety drug. They received a dummy pill that had no direct chemical effect on the body. In accordance with good practice, the students were informed of some of the expected benefits of the placebo, such as muscle relaxation and lower heart rate. They were also told about the potential side effects. These included headaches, nausea, dizziness and drowsiness.

Some students were given information that was framed negatively, with the emphasis on the number of people who could have negative experiences: 'Possible side effects include drowsiness. Approximately twenty-seven out of one hundred people will experience drowsiness.' The information was framed more positively for other students, with the emphasis on the number of people who would remain side-effect-free: 'Possible side-effects include drowsiness. However, seventy-three out of one hundred people will not experience drowsiness.'

The more information people have about side-effects, the more likely they are to experience them. These are known as nocebo effects and studies show that they are not imagined but result from significant shifts in hormones and neurotransmitters. Even though both groups were given the same statistical information, the research showed that a positive framing of the wording used changed the outcome.

Emotional Pain is a Wake-up Call

Reframing is a way of changing the way you think about something, and this has the potential to change your experience and your physical responses. In the research for his book *The Expectation Effect: How Your Mindset Can Transform Your Life*, David Robson found that many people taking placebo pills experience the benefits of the drug they believe they are taking. They also report having side-effects.

Current research shows that pain is your brain's way of signalling that something is wrong, something is amiss in the mind or body and needs attention. Normally, a broken leg will be severely painful and look swollen or bruised, but not always. A simple fall can fracture the lower leg bones and a broken bone in the leg may present as a pain in the knee or ankle. Someone with a fractured bone will be in a lot of pain, which may worsen with movement. Usually, doctors identify the root cause of acute pain before commencing treatment.

Our body's response to pain is triggered by what we perceive to be true. The body's stress response is triggered more often by perceived stress than by actual events. The body has the ability to produce endorphins and hormones that relieve pain, reduce stress and improve one's sense of wellbeing. Research shows that discomfort about a stressful event will ease when we are invited to think about a negative symptom in a more positive way.

What is not as widely recognised is that even if there is no physical damage to the body, your brain will generate pain signals to make you aware of the need to pay attention because something is amiss. The suffering caused by emotional pain is not imagined and can feel as stressful as physical pain. Acute stress is the type of stress we experience on a day-to-day basis, for example the stress of being late for an appointment or being stuck in heavy traffic.

Chronic stress could be described as the long-term emotional distress you feel when you are just about coping with daily life. When you have negative feelings about your future and lack the energy to take action that could potentially improve your situation, you have emotional pain that needs healing. If the brain experiences pain over and over again, neural pathways get strengthened and sensitised.

Pain is often the result of learned neural pathways in the brain and, just as pain can be learned, it can be unlearned. Neuroscientists tell us that physical and emotional pain is constructed entirely in the brain, which is capable of synthesising endorphins, natural opiates that can block pain. Football star Pepe played with a broken arm in his team's World Cup quarter-final loss to Morocco.

The magnitude of Tiger Woods's achievement in the last of his fourteen majors only became apparent after the full extent of the injury to his left knee was known. Even though Woods had torn the anterior cruciate ligament of his knee and had sustained a double stress fracture in his left tibia, he played his best and bravest tournament at Torrey Pines. He said, 'I couldn't have quit in front of all those people.'

The brain can generate intense physical pain even when there is no injury to the body. Pain expert Howard Schubiner tells of a construction worker who jumped down from scaffolding, landing on a large nail that pierced his boot. The man was in agony and was rushed to the hospital with the nail sticking out of the top of his boot. But when doctors removed the boot, they found that the nail had passed between two of his toes, without even causing a scratch. The nociceptor nerves that respond to damage or the possibility of damage to our bodies contribute to the sensation of pain. The construction worker's pain was intense when it appeared that there was a serious injury because the brain cannot differentiate between what is real and what we believe is real.

Pain functions as a danger signal generated by the brain so that we become aware that something is not right with the body, mind or spirit. The construction worker's brain generated the pain during the time he believed he was seriously hurt. His brain stopped generating the pain once it was clear that he was not injured. Even though the nail did not pierce his foot, the picture of the nail sticking out of the boot was the brain's signal to turn on the pain response. Your brain generates and controls emotion as well as physical pain. The mind can generate intense suffering without a physical source, or make pre-existing pain increase, linger or disappear.

A study at a Brisbane hospital examined children after they suffered burn injuries and found that a parent's reaction could either lessen or increase the child's pain. Adults have intuitively known this for generations. Our parents and grandparents didn't need research studies to prove that when a child's bleeding knee is kissed better, the child immediately stops crying. The child's belief that their mother or father can make pain go away is all that is necessary to turn tears into smiles.

At one time, it was believed that brains were static entities. A child's brain was pliable but the capacity of the brain to change was meant to disappear after adolescence. Since the 1990s, through meticulous research, neuroscientists have shown that this is not so. What you believe to be true has a powerful impact on your brain. The expectation of pain gives you pain. The benefits of taking a placebo are measurable.

Neuroplasticity is the brain's ability to form new neural pathways throughout life and in response to experiences. The brain's wiring is constantly changing. When you learn something new, a neural pathway is formed. A neural pathway is a series of connected neurons that send signals from one part of the brain to another. The more you think or use that neural pathway, the more dominant it becomes. If you don't practise it, the pathway is unused and your brain eventually 'disconnects' it.

The way your brain creates a neural pathway (a thought about something) can impact how you respond to that thing for the rest of your life because when you think of the thing in the same way repeatedly, it becomes your dominant neural pathway. When it comes to complex things, like emotions tied to thoughts, neural pathways help us to understand what may appear to be irrational fears.

Say for example, the first time you encountered a spider when you were a child, it really scared you, a neural pathway formed that linked spiders with fear. And if, for whatever reason, you continued having a fear response to spiders repeatedly, you might have grown up to be terrified of arachnids. Neural pathways can form negative associations.

A child who grows up afraid of a dominant male figure who shouts when angry may, as an adult, have what seems to be an irrational fear response to people who shout. The positive news is that your nervous system is neuroplastic, meaning you can rewire your brain and create new neural pathways. You can have a change of mind when you get new information that invites you to review old ideas.

As our neural pathways change, we learn and grow and develop as people. When a client who had arachnophobia, a fear of spiders, was guided through a Neuro Linguistic Phobia Cure exercise, he overcame his fear. When he was motivated by fear, the logical side of his brain could not assimilate the information that spiders are quite small and harmless eight-legged creatures. Once he overcame the fear, his perception changed and he was not afraid anymore.

It's wonderful to have new insights and a fresh outlook on life situations. Be tolerant and compassionate as you tune in to your expectations, examine your beliefs and do a reality check on what you say to yourself. It takes an effort to distinguish between facts and fiction, to drop your illusions and stop stifling your emotions.

Have you had the experience of feeling good in a situation when your partner felt bad and bad in a situation where your partner felt good? The life lesson is that it is not the situation you are in, but how you think about the situation that makes it feel good or bad for you.

3

TAKE RESPONSIBILITY FOR YOUR OWN HAPPINESS

The only person you are destined to become is the person you decide to be.

RALPH WALDO EMERSON

All relationships go through changes and changes can be exciting and disturbing at the same time. Even changes that are happily anticipated, such as moving in together, getting married, finding a new job, working from home or taking early retirement, are stressful.

Nothing in life is stable. Who you were at ten years of age will be different from who you were at twenty and different again from the person you are today. What makes you feel happy changes as you develop and mature. Your emotional needs change when you are with different people and in different situations. It's natural to find that you have lost interest and no longer take pleasure in things you once enjoyed.

What you need, want and desire alters as you develop and mature. Alterations in circumstance transform how you see yourself, whether you are aware of this or not. In subtle ways, becoming part of a couple, achieving a higher professional status, or losing your job can change your identity.

The perceptions you have about how you see yourself and how others relate to you are important for your self-esteem, wellbeing and confidence. In this context, the word 'self' refers to one's sense of 'who I am and what I am'. So, who are you? What you think, feel and choose to do affects who you think you are. Your sense of identity, who you believe you are, has an impact on how you expect to be treated. It would be wonderful if every person fully realised what motivated them to speak and act in the way they do. They don't.

In a utopian world, couples would speak honestly and directly to the truth of their experience. In the real world, only a very few partners have that freedom. The logical part of you may accept that it is next to impossible for even the most caring partner to be sensitive or aware of your unspoken desires and needs. Is it possible that the desire for your partner to meet your needs and wants could distract you from what you need to do for yourself?

The emotional part of you can desire to be loved so deeply that you want your partner to know what you need without being told. It may not be logical to experience a sense of disappointment when your partner does not give you what you never asked for in the first place. Logic doesn't always apply where emotions are concerned.

Admitting that you may have unrealistic expectations doesn't make coping any easier. If you are frustrated and angry with your partner, accept that you have genuine feelings of hurt and upset. Take an honest look at what triggered any negative feelings in you. It's likely that you will discover that you feel bad because you wanted something that you didn't get.

I have worked with many couples who transformed their relationship when they stopped playing 'the blame game'. The answer to the question, 'is it fair to expect a partner to live up to expectations that were never voiced?' is either 'no' or 'yes'. The challenging follow-up question when the answer is 'no' is, 'if your partner is not to blame, then who is responsible when you feel disappointed?' One insight that results from this interaction is that the client learns the important life lesson: I am responsible for my own happiness.

You have an emotional response to what you believe to be true, even if you have wrong or misleading information. Many of our beliefs are formed in childhood before the age of seven. Children are predisposed to believe their parents and authority figures. Unhelpful beliefs developed during childhood may linger in our subconscious mind and affect our emotions and behaviours.

Many of the beliefs you have about how you should be, how your partner should be and how you should treat each other are not even yours. Because your beliefs are so much a part of you, it's easy to assume your partner thinks as you do. Consider how your own expectations of your partner are influenced by what was modelled by your parents. This does not mean that you will necessarily repeat your parents' experiences, but what you observed in your childhood family will affect how you and your partner relate.

Your early experiences in childhood will be different from those of your partner. Some of these differences will be small and others will be considerably larger. Both will have an influence on differences in attitudes that you never thought about.

A simple explanation for why so many people do not have the kind of partnerships they want is they are not grounded in a sense of who they are. Some look to their partner for the love they rightly need to give to themselves. Others are so busy playing roles and people-pleasing that they have no idea who they are.

Bobby and Pat lived together for fifteen years before Pat became aware of how dissatisfied and unhappy he was at how they had settled into a dull routine. He came for coaching because he felt his partner should be more supportive and appreciative. For most of their relationship, Pat made Bobby's needs more important than his own. He believed that it was time for that to change. He felt upset that Bobby never expressed any appreciation for all his support.

Recognising that he was not good with words, Pat's perceived purpose in seeking communication coaching was to find an effective way to tell his partner he should put in more of an effort. He believed that Bobby was taking him for granted. He did not doubt that Bobby loved him and he was very clear that he was still in love. He wanted to stay with his partner for the rest of their lives and to grow old together, hopefully living in harmony.

It would have been unhelpful and counterproductive for me to explain what I discerned from Pat's use of the word 'should'. At some level, the use of the word 'should' implies that a person thinks they have the right to decide what ought to be done, how it ought to be done, and when it ought to be done. Usually, a person who uses the word 'should' is making a judgement. They believe that the way things are is not the way they want them to be, and that is a valid judgement.

Based on what they know or don't know, people believe they can determine what is right and wrong. You will read about the complexity of honest communication in another chapter. For now, it will suffice to point out that when you look at what is behind the layers of meaning in a single word like 'should', you may be surprised at what is uncovered or revealed.

You have some outcome in mind if you make a judgement that things 'should' be different. Perhaps there is a part of you that wishes that your partner would sense and know what you need to feel loved and lovable. Maybe you have a need to feel accepted and you make huge efforts to fit in and do what is expected of you. The need for acceptance is a basic human instinct but to meet this need some people make the decision to sublimate their wants and act nicer than they feel. Underneath the judgement that things should be different is a wish for control and unfulfilled desires.

Experiential understanding comes from engaging with the process of reflecting on questions that bring you deeper into your experience. In the exercise below, I will call what the client wishes to experience 'X':

- Think of just one thing you desire. It can be an emotion or an experience.
- For what purpose do you want to feel X?
- Why is that important?
- What will that do for you?

When I engage with a client in this exercise, I may repeat two questions a couple of times. When I get the answer to 'why is that important?' I take the exact words the client uses, let me call them 'Y', and I insert them in the question, 'What will 'Y' do for you?' Each time the questions are repeated, the client engages in a deeper level of introspection and self-reflection. Frequently, the answer to the final question is, 'I'll feel good about myself.'

Looked at from a professional perspective, someone who sets out to change another person is unconsciously seeking to manipulate or control the other person to some extent. As an ethical life coach, it was necessary for me to empower Pat to discover what he really needed, which was to focus on his own wants and needs, not on changing how his partner related to him.

In the fifteen years they were together, Pat and Bobby never had a conversation about their attitudes and expectations of each other. That didn't surprise me, as many people have clarity about what they don't want but are vague about what they wish for and need. To question beliefs that did not serve him well, I asked Pat if he was willing to be challenged and if he was prepared for probing questions, which he might find uncomfortable. 'Willing and able,' he quipped a little nervously.

I like wise old sayings such as, 'there are none as deaf as those who do not want to hear' and 'none as blind as those who do not want to see'. It would have been foolish and irresponsible of me to prematurely explain the implied obligations that lie with the use of the word 'should'.

He would have felt threatened by words such as 'judgement' and 'control'. Clients who feel threatened stop listening. However, when a client has an emotional experience that changes their perception of a personal situation, they gain insights that bring about a change in attitude, and frequently become aware of information they were blind to in the past.

Pat was perplexed when I asked him why he wanted Bobby to 'conform' to his expectations. He reacted negatively to the word 'conform'. If a client expresses a desire to have a partner behave in a way they consider more acceptable and avoid doing things they dislike or find upsetting, what they really want is for the other to conform to their expectations.

I looked for clarification to make sure I understood the situation. 'Pat, if I have this right, you believe that Bobby should be more supportive and appreciative. You think he should know better and treat you better. You want things to change. You are disappointed and have hurt feelings because you think you shouldn't be put in the position of having to ask Bobby. You know he loves you but from where you are looking today, he should be and could be doing better.'

I asked Pat to write down a detailed account of how their partnership would be different if I gave him a wand with magical powers. This wand could magic him into the kind of future relationship he desired and would allow him to imagine a picture of how the partnership between himself and Bobby would look five years into the future. In this scenario, he was to imagine they had ironed out all their differences and were living the way Pat felt they should be living.

The first direction was that each sentence should start with the words 'we would'. You might find this an interesting exercise to do for yourself. I wanted Pat to have an in-depth experience of the power of fantasy. In his imagination, he made up a story of how he wanted their future partnership to look. I told Pat not to hold back while he was writing; to forget about the limitations that might exist for him now. In his fantasy, he could allow himself to already have the communication skills that he came for coaching to learn. He could, if he wished, see Bobby as appreciative. It was important for him to have a clear picture of the changed partnership that he believed would make him happier and give him the good feelings he desired.

Once Pat finished writing, I asked him to go back over every sentence and connect with how he felt when he imagined the future that he created in his mind. This was a beautiful way for Pat to learn about the power of fantasy thinking. I didn't have to explain that the feelings he experienced while he was writing and reading his story were real. In doing the exercise, Pat gave himself the good feelings he wrongly believed he needed to get from his partner.

If you feel dissatisfied, please don't ignore your emotions.

Make the effort to identify why you feel upset, uncomfortable or discontented. Before you deal with a problem, it is useful to have a sense of who you are and to have clarity about how you feel. You may not like being asked to confront the truth about your partnership, but it is necessary.

Are you aware of the difference between something you need and what you want but can live without? Some people take the easy option when a partner asks, 'Is anything wrong?' Rather than explain what is wrong, they act as if everything is okay, which is lying by omission.

No one teaches you that lying by omission generates mistrust and gets in the way of you being authentically yourself. Many people believe that you can protect your partner from hurt, unaware that hiding the truth, even if the motive for doing so is positive, is controlling behaviour.

My criteria for what it means to be in an authentically loving relationship is to know who you are, accept what you know about yourself, and to be willing to share that information. To enjoy an intimate loving relationship, you need to be real, to be true to yourself and honest with your partner. Being totally honest is a monumental challenge because lying is endemic in society.

The perception that everyone tells little lies is widespread and has validity. Ignorance of the damage that lying to a partner has on a relationship is well-documented. A lie is a sign of fear and it is also a subtle means of control. What is your response to the sentence, 'you cannot truly love someone if you do not tell them the truth, the whole truth and nothing but the truth'? Does that sound like an idealistic but impractical idea? Or does it challenge you to hold yourself to a higher standard of integrity?

How clear are you about your personal values? Do you list honesty, integrity and kindness among them? I'm making an educated guess that out of kindness, you massage the truth. In plain English, your fear of telling the whole truth motivates you to control the information you share.

Lying is usually thought of as unethical, but in practice most people condone little white lies unaware that every time you tell a lie, you run the risk of damaging trust. There is very little that a person who is found out in lies can do to rebuild trust again.

To live authentically will take a lot of soul-searching and hard work. In the process, you will discover things about yourself that you have ignored, denied, avoided or refused to address. An important thing for you to be aware of on your quest for happiness is that self-acceptance is essential, if you desire to feel loved and lovable. I believe your happiness starts and ends with loving and accepting yourself exactly as you are and not as you would like to be.

Taking responsibility for your own happiness allows you to become the manager of your life. It empowers you to control and own every decision you make. One of the biggest obstacles to having what your heart desires is the stories you tell yourself to avoid facing the realities of life. When you feel uneasy about a decision or something just doesn't feel right, pause. Notice your thoughts and how you respond to what you are thinking. Experiment with changing your thoughts. When you change a thought, your feelings change.

Everything we do is experienced in our body, mind and spirit. If you act as if everything is all right when it is not, you are stifling your feelings. You may tell yourself that you are doing the right thing for the best of reasons. Making the best of a bad situation is not always good for you. It is not emotionally healthy to deny your so-called 'negative feelings'. Feelings are neither right nor wrong. They simply are.

I don't have to tell you that setting out to change yourself or your partner is a fool's errand. All I wish you would do is set out to understand yourself better. Seek to have clarity about why you do what you do; make the effort to reflect on why you want what you want; why you believe what you believe, and value what you value. Understanding will bring you clarity of perception and an accuracy of response.

You have some way of differentiating between your positive and negative feelings. Become aware of how you respond to a positive experience by naming the emotion. Say, for example, you look at two positive emotions, such as happy and fulfilled:

- How do I know I feel happy?
- How do I know I feel fulfilled?
- What am I aware of physically in my body when I am happy?
- What am I aware of physically in my body when I am feeling fulfilled?
- How do I distinguish the difference between these two positive emotions?

Think of two negative emotions such as fear and anger and ask:

- How do I know I feel fear?
- How do I know I feel anger?
- What am I aware of physically in my body when fear is in me?
- What am I aware of physically in my body when anger is in me?

- How do I distinguish the difference between fear and anger?

Are you wondering why I said, when fear is in me, when anger is in me? Emotions start as sensations in the body. For this exercise, I'm going to suggest that feelings are how we interpret our emotions. There's a constant feedback loop between your body and mind, known as the mind-body connection.

When I tell myself 'I'm afraid', I'm identifying with the emotion I named and ignoring all the other feelings that are in me which overlap. There is a popular belief that you can only feel one emotion at a time, but this is not so. For example, excitement, sadness and happiness are feelings that don't match up and sound as if they would be in conflict, but overlap and can be present with fear or anger.

Do not be surprised if you find the questions about negative emotions much easier to answer than the ones about positive experiences. Connecting the emotions of anger to physical feelings in the body seems to be a common experience, whereas identifying the physical sensations that indicate the labels you put on other emotional states can be more challenging.

This may be a good time to pause and spend time with the narratives you have given credence to about the actions and motives of your partner. Becoming aware of what you are thinking means paying attention to facts and fantasies. Facts do not change. The stories you tell yourself about why you are getting or not getting what you desire contain an element of fantasy. I've suggested to clients that they use words such as 'illusion' or 'hallucination' rather than 'fantasy' for their narratives.

A fantasy relies on imagination, emotion and intuition, without logic or any constraints. Think of your internal dialogue as a fantasy, a narrative about a story you tell yourself, but it exists only in your mind. You react to this illusion as if everything in the narrative is the gospel truth. You identify partly with your own feelings and partly with the fantasy narrative you believe to be true; the emotional response to what you think is real, even though it may or may not be true.

How frequently do you focus on what you value and appreciate rather than on what is lacking in your partnership? Take advice from one of the great spiritual masters, Anthony de Mello, SJ, who said, 'it's impossible to be unhappy and have a grateful heart'.

One of the ways we define ourselves is through our relationships with others. Moving in with a partner or getting married changes your single status. When circumstances in people's lives change, they find ways to adjust to the changes but always with some degree of struggle.

You may think you know yourself but are you aware that if you change careers, become a parent or retire, you will need to adjust to major changes in how you see yourself? Labels such as 'manager', 'parent' or 'retiree' define roles. It's good to be open to the idea that a change in status may alter the relationship you have with yourself, your partner and your extended family in ways you could never have anticipated.

The Covid-19 pandemic had a monumental impact worldwide. It changed people's perceptions, priorities and future plans. Whether you were with a partner for five months, five years or fifty years, being confined during lockdown affected your couple relationship for good or ill.

The gift for some partners was the recognition of the depth of their love. The wake-up call for others was the uncomfortable revelation that they had a functional partnership that was focused on practical day-to-day activities. Partners who were working from home and unable to socialise were forced to face up to problems they had denied or ignored. Some had allowed life to get so busy their relationship was neglected.

A couple's sex life is a good barometer of the state of their partnership because it mirrors their satisfaction with other aspects of their relationship. When partners are not having sex, the level of intimacy and emotional connection are significantly decreased. Going for long periods without sex can cause a person to feel undesirable or rejected.

Having a facility with words and being able to express one's ideas clearly is of little help when it comes to having a conversation about sensitive issues like sex. Talking about your need for intimacy involves risk. It takes courage to be honest about what you like your partner to do or to disclose what you think of as an unusual desire.

We had no role models to teach us the appropriate language or suggest how to introduce this kind of conversation. Performance anxiety, issues around pornography, fear of rejection and body insecurities are obstacles to having this difficult but necessary dialogue

Do you accept that your partner can not give you what you never requested? Are you aware of the ambivalence in you when your emotional needs are not met and perhaps you resent your partner for this? There are many different parts in you. A part of you may understand why you have a negative response to unspoken expectations that you kept from your partner and another part of you may resent this and react negatively.

There are many reasons for why partners are dissatisfied with each other. Women can secretly feel cheated of the intimacy, passion and romance they once enjoyed and are now missing. The deterioration in their sex life or the lack of sex is what tends to alert men to their own dissatisfaction.

In an authentically loving, secure and trusting relationship, partners enjoy the freedom to be themselves. They feel loved and accepted for who they are. They feel safe to talk about their needs, to ask for what they want from each other and are comfortable to tell the truth about how they cope or don't cope with emotions.

To adjust to living with someone involves compromise and flexibility, which are two of the most important resources in a loving, enduring partnership. Are you aware of your partner's attitudes to, and expectations of you? Don't be too hasty to say 'yes'.

You may be sharing the same home with the partner you were with on this day last year but right now you are not the same two people. You have had life experiences and learning that changed how you think, feel and act. When you are with your partner, who do you relate to, the person who is here and present today or the person you fell in love with, who no longer exists?

Many couples enjoy routine lives. People fall in love, decide to move in together, and, for a time, enjoy the experience of living happily and contentedly together. They have minor disagreements but few major rows and at a surface level they are content until an unexpected change in circumstances happens and puts pressure on the relationship.

Have you the freedom to talk to your partner about all that is going on in your life or do you hold information back? The decision not to share how you feel or to explain how your partner has contributed to your feelings sets a precedent. How clear are you about what you want or do not want or desire in your relationship? Flexibility and honest communication are the keystones for a happy partnership that meets the needs of both partners.

If this strikes a chord, it may be helpful to pause and answer this challenging question: In the bedroom, who are you, a lover, pleasure-seeker, partner or soulmate? In a different context, when I ask this question, clients assume that they have answered me when they say their name. But you are not your name.

Please allow me to ask a question that is useful for reflection: Who are you? I don't want to know your name. I want to know *who* you are. I don't want to know that you are someone's partner or a good friend or a loving person. I am not interested in what you do for a living. My question is, who are you?

Seek to discover if the part of you that yearns for your partner to meet your needs and wants could be blinding you to what you need to do for yourself. Stay on the quest for happiness and find out who you really are and why you react the way that you do.

4

CONTINUED INFLUENCE EFFECT

Progress is impossible without change, and those who cannot change their minds cannot change anything.

GEORGE BERNARD SHAW

Do you have a sense of autonomy? Do you have the freedom to act in your own interests, and honour your values without feeling selfish? In other words, do you experience a sense that you have control over your life? Taking control over your life does not mean you control everything that happens. It means embracing the belief that you have the freedom to think your own thoughts and respond with your own feelings.

Author and motivational speaker Jack Canfield said, 'You only have control over three things in your life – the thoughts you think, the images you visualise, and the actions you take (your behaviour). How you use these three things determines everything you experience. If you don't like what you are producing and experiencing, you can change your responses.'

American industrialist and businessman Henry Ford said, 'Whether you think you can or you think can't, you're right.' A good first step if you are serious about wanting to have autonomy is to become aware of what you are thinking about yourself. Is your internal dialogue caring, compassionate and tolerant? Do you encourage your own efforts with a 'can do' attitude? Do you think of yourself as a victim of circumstances which could make you feel powerless, fearful to take any action that might upset others?

You may not be aware that words like 'can' and 'can't' have the potential to empower progress or to be a huge obstacle to taking action as you set out on the journey to have more control over your life. Take a moment to think about how using one four-letter word such as 'can't' might keep you stuck. The expectations when you think you can't do something are like the ending to a Christian prayer: as it was in the beginning, is now and ever shall be.

Add the word 'yet' and you will free yourself from feeling stuck. 'I can't yet' suggests that in the future, if you take action, go to a class, research on Google, listen to a podcast, and find some way to build your skill set, you can succeed. With a 'can do' attitude you will identify, probe and question your motivation. If you are willing, you can identify the limiting beliefs that put obstacles in your path. Isn't it astonishing that adding or changing even one word in a sentence will open up endless opportunities that alter your expectations?

Do you have clarity about what stops you from having the quality of life you desire? Is it lack of self-esteem, a victim attitude, a skills deficit, a lack of ambition, or wrong beliefs that you never thought to question? Emotional self-awareness is essential for success in every sphere of life. If you don't know how you feel and why you feel the way you do, you will lack the self-knowledge that is needed to feel you have control over what you choose to think and feel.

At our core, we want to feel loved and lovable but misinformation, the flawed and limiting beliefs we assume are true, stop us from feeling the way we believe we should be feeling. Although people are quick to dismiss what they think of as fake news, they are much slower to recognise when they have wrong beliefs that do not serve them well.

If you believe that wrong information can easily be corrected by providing relevant facts, you are wrong. Misinformation can often continue to influence people's thinking even after they receive a correction and accept the correction is true. This tenacity is known as the Continued Influence Effect (CIE). When information is encoded into memory and when new information that discredits it is learned, the original information is not simply erased or replaced. Instead, misinformation and corrective information coexist and compete for activation.

Drinkers often ignore current suggestions for the moderate use of alcohol for healthy adults despite knowing that excessive alcohol use can lead to the development of chronic diseases and other serious problems.

In a study that looked at how emotion influences us, it was found that corrections can produce psychological discomfort that motivates a person to disregard the correction to reduce the feeling of discomfort. When your life experience discredits beliefs that are encoded into memory, the original information is not erased, which explains why so many people have an idealised fantasy of living happily with a partner.

Poor judgement is only partly responsible for the negative feelings people experience when reality fails to match up to what they hoped to experience. The information one gets on an internet search may be accurate, inaccurate, biased or outdated. Governments do not put enough resources into spotting fake accounts and detecting campaigns that spread false and misleading information. Do not underestimate how your beliefs are affected by media influences, misinformation and fables.

Young people are learning to detect and filter the false and misleading information that many adults who are not as well-informed about media influences unquestioningly accept as factual. Even children know that the fairy tales where two people meet, fall in love, get married and live happily ever after are myths. Romantic stories bear little relationship to reality but they influence and contribute to the expectations people have of how life will be with a partner.

Media stories, though compelling, do not provide strong evidence of how celebrities relate when the cameras are off and they no longer feel the need to be on their best behaviour. The challenge for viewers and readers is to apply critical thinking. How do you distinguish between what you perceive happier couples enjoy and what you assume is lacking in your life? Is it wise to believe that anecdotes and personal stories, no matter how convincing they may seem, reflect reality?

Unrealistic expectations amplified by social media are currently affecting people who compare the mundane relationships they judge they have with the perceived mind-blowing joy and bliss exhibited by couples they see on social media or follow online. Compared to the idealised hyped-up media accounts of 'perfect couples', there is a lack of romance between most long-term partners.

An interesting exercise is to look at your own life from the perspective of either party in what you label as 'a happier couple'.

Life is a series of gains and losses. Say, for example, you admired the slender figure, immaculate grooming and beautiful clothes of a female celebrity. If the roles were reversed, the gains for her could be the freedom from spending over an hour on hair and make-up each morning, getting away from the glare of publicity and having the space to chill out and relax. The loss of her glamorous image and adoring fans might be a price she would be willing to pay to gain autonomy over her life and enjoy the benefits of the life you regard as mundane.

From the perspective of a life coach, it's fascinating to observe how quickly a client can have a change of mind when given a reality check. Few people understand how much power our unrealistic thoughts and expectations have to generate poor judgements, disappointment and dissatisfaction. Three simple questions – What are you thinking? How are you feeling? Where does that feeling come from? – will bring about a change in basic assumptions in thinking. When a client experiences how their thoughts generate their feelings, it transforms their understanding and they find themselves challenged to adapt to a new way of looking at themselves and life events.

The glut of lifestyle magazines and social media portraying seemingly blissfully happy couples and the conversations that are sparked from the coverage are catalysts for building up unrealistic expectations of what it means to be happy in a partnership, a marriage or a family. It's wise to be discerning about what you assume about other people's relationships. Judging only by appearance is not a great idea. The street angel who behaves exemplarily in company but behind closed doors or after a few drinks becomes the house devil – rude, disrespectful and abusive – is far more common than most people realise.

A worthwhile exercise is to reflect on what you appreciate and value about your relationship with your partner. You may have different love languages. Be open-minded. Many clients discover that by taking a partner's acts of service or words of affirmation for granted, they failed to value the expressions of love demonstrated in either words or actions. You might find that some of the things you look on as negative in your current relationship are based on unrealistic expectations, assumptions and wrong beliefs that you were not aware of before now.

Would you want to recognise, correct and challenge beliefs

that limit your happiness? The logical part of you is likely to say 'yes' but there are many other parts of you that will hold on to habits, routines and programmed beliefs that you have never questioned. People are always looking for evidence to support their unexamined beliefs. Even when the contradictory evidence is quite literally staring them in the face, they will simply choose to dismiss it rather than update their beliefs.

Say Kathy's in-laws are coming to dinner. Her narrative is that she must drop children off at two different schools, shop for fresh vegetables, buy cream, text her partner to pick up the dry cleaning and as soon as she gets to work, she has three urgent phone calls to make. She berates herself for being an idiot because she can't remember where she put her keys.

Forgetting where she put the keys does not make Kathy an idiot. It makes her a victim of her own negative self-talk. In that situation, a person with more self-awareness might say something like, 'I'm not comfortable about cooking for the in-laws; I feel under pressure because I have so much to do to prepare a family meal; it's hardly surprising that I failed to remember where I put my keys.'

Dropping self-blame can make a monumental difference to self-esteem. Improved self-esteem allows self-confidence to grow and as a person becomes aware of an improved sense of self-worth, they feel better, happier and more content.

Kathy forgot where she put her keys because she was under time pressure and apprehensive about all she had to do. Some may wrongly put her stress down to having to shop and cook for her in-laws. Their visit may have triggered this response in her but her dinner guests deserve no blame for her emotional state.

We can only guess at why she had a long list of tasks on her 'to do list' and why she had not given herself enough time to do them in comfort. Perhaps she overslept, which did not allow sufficient time for the tasks involved or she had a history of being over-committed or she wanted to make a good impression on her guests by using fresh produce in her cooking.

Accepting responsibility for how you act and feel in different circumstances will challenge you to be alert to misinformation that generates negative thoughts, inaccurate judgements and unpleasant feelings. Understanding how to take responsibility for your own emotions in circumstances where you once believed other people put you under pressure is a life-changing insight.

It is said that the best predictor of future experiences is past experience. Our brains evolved to make predictions drawing on our past experiences, observations of others and our cultural norms – a process that underlies our perceptions of reality. Whether we are totally relaxed or under enormous pressure, what we believe to be true shapes our emotional responses in every circumstance. If a person makes harsh judgements, is intolerant and lacks self-understanding, this can chip away at their sense of self-worth and damage their self-esteem.

Each of us would do well to make the decision to be kinder and more compassionate to ourselves. Be more tolerant with yourself to take back control over your life and connect with who you are. You have always and in every circumstance done the best you could with the information you had at the time. Be realistic when you look back and feel frustration or regret for situations you wished you had handled differently. With hindsight, you have the benefit of knowing the outcome of the actions you took; but if you were back in any situation with the emotional state you were in and with the information you had at that time, you could not have made a different decision.

Learn to separate fact from fantasy. Be alert to programmed thinking and practise being kind, compassionate and tolerant with yourself. Develop an awareness of where your thinking comes from. Is it from you or from your programming? Decide to consciously set out to love and accept yourself exactly as you are and not as you assume others want you to be. Many people find the sentiments of the Serenity Prayer very helpful. They ask for the grace to accept the things they cannot change, the courage to change the things they can and the wisdom to know the difference.

It is unrealistic to expect to change a lifetime of programmed thinking overnight. Change takes self-awareness, time, effort and motivation, which are limited resources. Any time that we feel disheartened and judge that our best efforts are not good enough, it's probably because our willpower to resist impulses is depleted and our self-control is exhausted.

Most of us are familiar with the internal conflict when one part of us wants to do something and the other part doesn't. Until recently, it was believed that using willpower and self-control are all one needs to change habitual patterns of behaviour. Psychologists have discovered that self-control is an exhaustible resource. It's not unlike bench presses. The first one is easy when your muscles are fresh. But with each additional repetition, your muscles get more exhausted until you can't lift the bar.

Developments in neuroscience over the last thirty years have revolutionised our understanding of the brain. People don't stick with their goals because when it comes to changing behaviour, humans tend to act somewhat irrationally. The rational part of our brain usually wants something very different to the emotional part. For a person who struggles with weight, resisting the temptation to eat a chocolate bar can use up most of that day's supply of willpower.

The conventional wisdom in psychology is that the brain has two independent systems always working. The rational side deliberates analyses and looks to the future. The emotional side looks for the instant gratification of eating the chocolate over the long-term goal of sticking with the diet and coming down a dress size.

In his book, *The Happiness Hypothesis*, psychologist Jonathan Haidt, from the University of Virginia, compares our emotional side to an elephant and our rational side to its rider. The rider seems to be in charge when he holds the reins; but if the six-tonne elephant and the rider disagree about which way to go, the elephant wins. The elephant's hunger for instant gratification is the opposite of the rider's strength to plan for the future.

The problem, when the rider and elephant have different mindsets about which way to go, is the rider can only tug on the reins hard enough to make the elephant submit for a short time. He won't succeed in the longer term because in a tug of war with the elephant, the rider will become exhausted.

If your rational side is motivated to change behaviour but your emotional side is not ready, you're caught up in a tug of war that generates internal turmoil. Haidt explains that when our best efforts to stay focused on the goal fail, it's because the rider can't keep the elephant on the road for long enough to reach the desired destination.

Be realistic about recognising the efforts you make when progress is slow or you reach a plateau. Some people are in the habit of making a kind of half-hearted apology: 'I know I really shouldn't' when they treat themselves to the bar of chocolate or glass of wine. Unless the person has diabetes or an alcohol addiction issue, there is no logic to denying oneself pleasure once the decision is made to have a treat.

If you feel disheartened and think that your best efforts are not good enough, it's probably because your willpower to resist impulses is depleted and your self-control is exhausted. If you're mentally and emotionally ready to make a short-term sacrifice, for a long-term goal, you'll feel energised by success.

Be tolerant with yourself when you fail to live up to your own expectations, as at times you probably will. On the days that you are so frustrated with yourself that you feel like you want to give up, recognise that this is simply a blip, a minor setback. It certainly doesn't mean that you've failed. You have probably asked too much of yourself. Could you break a long-term goal into a series of smaller goals that are easier to achieve? Success builds on success.

Be confident in your ability to have a sense of autonomy. Know that you always have the power to reframe and reinterpret your thoughts. Changing how you feel emotionally is a decision. It becomes easier once you develop the awareness of how perceptions change when you connect with new information. Once you accept that you can do this, are determined that you will do this, and you will not stop yourself, you are in possession of the keys to success.

Often when I ask a client, 'What specifically do you want?' they are surprised at their own lack of clarity. It's very easy to say, 'I want to be happy'; it's harder to answer the question, 'How specifically do you know you are happy?' Some people list off behaviours, such as smiling, laughing or wearing a big grin, which are the physical expressions of a happy person. Others admit that they simply do not know.

Everybody wants to feel happy, but our ideas of what makes

us feel happy are forever changing. The thought that change needs to happen may be an accurate reflection of where you are in your life. Couples in enduring partnerships learn how to adjust and adapt to their own changing needs and to family circumstances. This is where it gets complex. If you lack clarity about what needs to improve, if you don't have criteria for what will make you happy, how can you feel fulfilled, content or at peace with yourself?

If your relationship with your partner is not the way you want it to be, if you are not as happy as you desire to be, is it possible that you lack clarity about what specifically you want? Could it be that you have made comparisons and judgement based on unexamined beliefs? It's astonishing how frequently intelligent people believe that if only they could get their partner to do what they need and want them to do, they would feel much happier. At the surface level, this may seem like an acceptable desire, but look a little deeper, and you will find there are hidden control issues.

Couple relationships work two ways and if one person is unhappy and dissatisfied, the other partner will be negatively affected. It must be uncomfortable to be around an unfulfilled person, who is aware that something is lacking in their partnership but is unable to say what specifically that is. There are two possible answers to the question 'Do you believe your partner makes you happy?'. There is no room for ambiguity. Answer either 'yes' or 'no'.

People who answer 'yes' have wrong information and wrong beliefs that are the root cause of many of the difficulties they experience in life. If a person can make you happy, they can also make you sad. You would not willingly give another person the power to control your emotions, but in effect that is what very many of us do. Control issues are complex and it may be difficult to accept that they exist in every relationship we have – with our partner, our parents and our friends.

Controlling someone or allowing yourself to be controlled probably goes against your values. If you pause to look at what is under your desire to feel happy and content, you will likely find you desire more control. A part of you wants to be free to do what you want to do, when you want to do it and to feel you have full control over every aspect of your life. Another part has commitments and obligations that you feel duty-bound to meet.

In reality, you are already in control. You are the manager of your own emotional life and you can do an exercise to prove it to yourself right now. Write down a list of five things that you believe you must do in a brief sentence. For example:

- I have to put petrol in the car.
- I have to shop for groceries.
- I have to make dinner.
- I have to bring bottles to the bottle bank.
- I have to tidy my bedroom.

Take a moment to get a sense of how you feel when you tell yourself you have to do these things. Notice if you feel any tension or anxiety. Then change 'I have to' to 'I want to', keeping the same list. For example:

- I want to put petrol in the car.
- I want to shop for groceries.
- I want to make dinner.
- I want to bring bottles to the bottle bank.
- I want to tidy my bedroom.

Take a moment to get a sense of how you feel when you tell yourself you want to do the same tasks. Do you feel the same as when 'you had to' or different? Most clients experience a difference. If your belief is that you should, must or ought to do something, a part of you feels controlled from an external source. The phrase 'I want to' puts you in control. If you have a choice, your emotional response changes. The freedom to choose is empowering.

Has anyone ever explained to you why you can feel good in a bad situation and bad in a good situation? A person who stifles their feelings and acts as if everything is all right when it's not is hiding who they are. They may have a sense of satisfaction about how they learned to cope but at what cost? My understanding is that you cannot be true to yourself when you wear a mask and act nicer than you feel.

There are many reasons why a partner may decide to go through the motions of putting on a happy face but inside feel sad, disappointed, and dissatisfied. The wear and tear of issues that arise from the daily grind always takes a toll. Some partnerships are strengthened when couples face problems together. Other couples carry on as if the problems didn't exist, as if they will magically disappear of their own accord. Issues need to be faced together if a partnership is to endure.

Fear of one's own and one's partner's feelings is often an obstacle for someone who would like to make a genuine effort to deal with problems but lacks the courage to do so. Issues will only come between you and your partner if you let them.

I could tell you that each time you face a problem and come through it, your courage will grow, your self-confidence will be strengthened, and you give yourself a great opportunity to prove that you can overcome the obstacles in your path. I would rather you discover this for yourself. On the quest for happiness, self-knowledge is the key to building self-confidence, self-esteem, self-worth, and celebrating who you are.

5

Is it You or Your Programming?

Every small positive change we make in ourselves repays us in confidence in the future.

ALICE WALKER

The most famous speech in William Shakespeare's play, *As You Like It* begins with 'All the world's a stage, and all the men and women merely players'. You play many roles in life, that of a child, a friend, a student, a partner, a lover, a colleague, a neighbour, etc. Your programmed brain has unwritten instructions on how to act with different people and in all sorts of situations.

Most of us are programmed to put on a brave face to mask our insecurities when we feel uneasy or uncertain about how to act. Any time you wear a mask or play a role, you are bound to feel insecure. People can only relate to the role you play but not to who you are. The mask you wear to hide your vulnerabilities stops you being authentic, which builds up feelings of insecurity. This gives rise to the fear that if people really knew who you were, they might reject you. Such fears grow exponentially.

Few of us realise that everything we do is experienced by our whole being, body and soul, heart and mind, memory and imagination. Hardly anyone pays attention to the twinge of inner conflict they experience when making a decision. There are many different parts in you and you experience inner turmoil when your parts want different things and you are emotionally pulled in different directions.

If you want to be truly happy and content, you want all levels of your body, mind and spirit to be in harmony. When you experience an uncomfortable feeling, please pay attention to your own narrative. Check for facts in the stories you tell yourself. As you develop an awareness of the role your mind and imagination play in the conversations you have with yourself, you will begin to recognise when you are unconsciously motivated by your programmed thinking. When you gain new insights, your thinking will change. This alters how you feel and it also influences what you believe.

Between the ages of two and three, children start to play pretend. Toddlers act out familiar routines such as feeding a doll with a bottle or putting their teddy to bed. Role play is a powerful educational tool where children learn to use their imaginations and creativity. It's fun for them to try out different roles, to play mummies and daddies, to act like a superhero, or become an explorer or a popstar. Through playing with other children, they learn how to cope with new situations.

In pretend games, children learn communication skills and how to co-operate and collaborate with other children in their make-believe role plays. Sadly, bullying and aggressive behaviour start at a very early age. Toddlers will fight to defend their possessions, territory, and friendships. From the uncertainty and chaos of childhood games, children develop beliefs about themselves and their capabilities.

The narrative of the preschool child who is last to be picked for an activity, or the child who feels bullied by a bossy friend, or the younger sibling who doesn't understand the rules of a game, may go something like, 'I'm not as good as the other children. I don't fit in. I'm not wanted'. You may discover if you listen with the eyes and ears of your childhood self that to protect yourself from being teased, you learned to put on a brave face and mask your feelings from a very young age.

When role-play is used with adults in skills training and therapeutic settings, it provides a safe opportunity to explore, investigate, and experiment with different ways of dealing with real-life issues. In a group setting, it illustrates how people engage, collaborate or distance themselves from others. Regardless of age, there is a value for children and adults to rehearse roles that they may play out in the future. Acting out real-life events offers opportunities to explore and test out life choices in a safe space.

Role-playing is a powerful tool for people of all ages. It is of enormous help in teaching us to understand ourselves, and in setting realistic goals for what we want in the future. Imagine changing the beliefs that block your happiness and prevent you from living life to the full. If you didn't feel the need to do the expected thing, would your life look and feel different? In what way would it be different?

If you wish, you could try an exercise to find out. Do not underestimate the power of using your imagination to visualise what your heart desires. Your brain cannot distinguish between what is real and what is an illusion and fantasy. In a role play, you can decide who you are now and who you want to be in the future.

Is it exciting or scary to imagine how your life would change if you had the confidence to love and accept yourself exactly as you are, warts and all? Have you any concept of what it would feel like? How would it be to neither fear nor care if anyone discovered whatever it is that you would prefer that people never found out about you? Suppose you could give yourself the freedom to be authentically who you are, no holds barred.

Would you look the same as you do now or do you imagine that you would look somewhat different?

You could, if you wish, visualise yourself five years in the future. Imagine this future you is in an emotionally healthy place. You look confident, have integrity, and are open, honest and vulnerable. Defensiveness is a thing of the past. The walls are down and the future you is relaxed, confident, free and comfortable. Your present self intuits that it is a genuine confidence and comes from deep inside.

Visualise the changed body language. Pay close attention to the posture, the eyes, and the facial expression of this confident being. Now step into this image and become this person. Experience what it feels like. Feel free to ask the future you how to become who you want to be. Write down the words you hear. This is the best advice you will ever get.

There is no right or wrong way to do this exercise. You are the only person who knows why you react as you do to any person or situation. Bear in mind that feelings are situation-specific. Your feelings change when your mood or perceptions change. At the beginning of relationships, most of us present our best selves. This gives a partner unrealistic expectations of who we are.

The man who believed his partner loved to go to football matches with him when they were dating may feel deceived when she makes an admission: she likes but never loved football. When she said she wanted to go to matches with him, her explanation had the ring of truth. She was so in love and wanted to be with him that she would have gone to the moon to be in his company. I agree with the old saying, 'The truth will set you free'.

People are constantly evolving. As each person becomes

self-aware and understands themselves better, they will learn how even tiny changes have the potential to make a welcome difference. Let's take this one step at a time: Two people in a relationship need to grow and evolve individually to grow as a couple. It is likely that they will grow apart before they come back together with a stronger, more loving and intimate partnership.

It's fascinating to figure out how something you once enjoyed no longer gives you pleasure. A trait that you found endearing in a partner at one time may grate like a pebble in the shoe later. A joke that may seem hilarious with one set of friends may turn out to be excruciatingly embarrassing with another. No two people react in the same way to the same situation.

The first conscious reaction some people are aware of is an emotion. For others, it could be a physical sensation or a thought. The order in which you become aware of what is happening in you is not important. What is important is that you pay attention to all three: what you are thinking, what you are feeling physically in your body, and how you are feeling emotionally.

Are you in control of what you are thinking, what you are feeling emotionally, and how your thoughts affect how you feel physically in your body? Or could it be that it is your programmed thinking that is in control? Your subconscious mind consists of long-term memory, emotions, feelings, habits and behaviour patterns. It acts like a giant memory bank in which all your memories, emotions and beliefs about everything you have ever experienced get stored, like how programmes are stored on a computer. When you act without thinking about what you are doing, it's usually because you have done it many times before and you are acting on auto-pilot.

Science estimates that ninety-five per cent of our brains' activity is unconscious. Most of the decisions we make, the actions we take, our emotions and behaviours, depend on the ninety-five per cent of brain activity that lies beyond conscious awareness. Our subconscious mind is like a computer programme that drives all the behaviours we do automatically.

If you go through your morning routine half-asleep, you are working on auto-pilot. If you hear words coming out of your mouth, and you find yourself wondering why you said something, it's because you were working on auto-pilot. Your computer brain keeps your heart beating, your body breathing and your blood flowing through your veins.

It's interesting to learn how little your thinking brain is in control. You don't have to think about how to wake-up, breathe or open your eyes. You do all of this on auto-pilot. Imagine how much time it would take if you had to figure out how to move your muscles to sit up and work out how to get out of bed. All of this occurs without thinking, and in much the same way as what we do physically is done on automatic pilot, much of what we think and feel and how we react is also conducted on automatic pilot without any conscious awareness on our part.

It's challenging to accept that you create your perceptions of the world and react to them emotionally, whether they are accurate or not. You react to what you believe to be true because your brain is unable to distinguish between what is real and what is an illusion or a fantasy. Some of the limiting beliefs you have about yourself date back to an incident in your childhood when you were under seven years of age.

If your partner is late and hasn't texted you to let you know what caused the delay, how do you react? Do you make assumptions about the reason for the delay? Of course you do.

Do your thoughts allow you to feel justified in getting frustrated or angry? Is it normal to react this way with someone who doesn't have the courtesy to explain why you were left waiting? For some people, the answer is 'yes', for others it is 'no'.

We all know people who imagine the worst possible outcome in a situation. Some people panic if their partner is five minutes late. They consciously hold on to the belief that if they imagine the worst, if it is not as bad as they think it could be, they have saved themselves emotional distress. They feel energised when things turn out better than they expected. Others wait to find out what happened before they react.

If you have incomplete information, your brain fills in the gaps and offers a narrative based on what you believe to be true. Whether what you tell yourself is accurate or not, your emotions are real. Your guesses, your explanation, your internal dialogue all evoke feelings that are very real for you, even if what you are reacting to exists only in your mind. If you are unaware of how you create your perceptions of the world, you may also be unaware of how you learned to blame others for negative feelings that are self-generated.

You always have an explanation for why you feel emotionally upset. However, what appears logical to you may look like poor judgement to someone else. Anne is aware that she panics in all sorts of situations where other people stay calm. Intellectually, she understands that there are simple techniques she could use to keep herself calm. She knows how to slow her breathing. She understands the theory of cognitive behavioural therapy. Yet she constantly worries about things that never happen.

Anne is like many people who don't want to change even when they have the knowledge and the tools to do so. What they want is to be made comfortable with their pain. Anne believes her mother was a worrier, and she inherited that trait. Her perception is that worrying is in her DNA. Nothing I say will change her mind because she has convinced herself that as it was in the beginning, is now and ever shall be. She is right because we create what we believe in.

For her, the discomfort of breaking the habits of a lifetime outweighs the benefits of thinking in a new way. Anne has a programmed response that has become a habit that she is unwilling to break. The personal work and effort involved in cultivating new ways of thinking and behaving are too much for her at this time in her life.

Her brain is programmed to think in a very different way to my brain. If a friend brought me a beautiful bouquet of flowers on the day that I had a letter telling me that I won seventy-five euro in a prize bond draw, I would think my luck was in. This happened to Anne and I could hardly believe my ears when I heard her say, 'That's my luck for the year gone.'

Inaccurate, limiting, and wrong beliefs are at the root of much negative thinking. Some negative habits are easier to break than others. Cognitive Behavioural Therapy (CBT) is a well-studied mental health treatment for training the brain to think differently. It empowers people suffering with anxiety or clinical depression to create long-lasting change. Neuro-Linguistic Programming (NLP) practitioners comment on the language used by clients. The words used in self-talk can damage self-confidence and generate stress. When the benefits of a change in thinking are experienced, the motivation to seek a more positive approach is powerful.

There are ways to train your brain to think differently when you become aware that you engage in self-sabotaging behaviours. Say for example that you love food and are determined to do something about your weight but chocolate is your downfall. You see a bar of chocolate and your conscious mind says, 'Don't eat it; you're looking at a calorie bomb.' Another part encourages you to 'Go on and eat it. Treat yourself. You know you deserve it.' The internal dialogue is exhausting. One part of you says, 'You'll regret it if you do' and the other part says, 'You'll regret it if you don't'.

Grown-ups have mixed feelings that often generate internal conflicts carried over from childhood beliefs. You experience internal conflict if a part of you puts chocolate in the category of junk food, which you consider unhealthy, while another part sees it as a treat and loves the taste. If chocolate was a childhood treat, it belongs to the category of 'feel-good foods' which are filed in your 'instant reward, pleasure and comfort reaction' programme.

You have internal rules that guide how you think, feel and act. There is an odd kind of logic to taking pleasure in something that you know you will later regret. There are many different parts of you that pull you in different directions. It's as if your computer brain has several different programmes running in your subconscious at the same time and, when there is internal conflict, the desire for instant gratification usually wins.

More than fifty per cent of people make New Year's resolutions to lose weight. Virtually every study tells us that around eighty per cent of these resolutions will be abandoned by February, possibly by people who are exhausted from trying too hard. When we feel disheartened and think that our best efforts are not good enough, it's probably because our willpower to resist impulses is depleted and our self-control is exhausted.

The rational part of our brain usually wants something very different to the emotional part. When you're mentally and emotionally ready to make a short-term sacrifice (not eat the chocolate) for a long-term goal (feeling slimmer and healthy), you will be energised by success. Success builds on success and you will be pleasantly surprised at how quickly you discover that when you have accurate information and experiential understanding, it will make changes in thought and action so much easier than you anticipated.

Being tolerant and compassionate with yourself brings clarity of perception that invites forgiveness and self-acceptance. When you are intolerant with yourself, you are focused on what you don't want and this makes it more likely that the unwanted behaviour will reoccur. You could cultivate the habit of practising awareness, of paying attention to what you are thinking, what you are feeling emotionally and physically, and gain great enjoyment from the experience.

There are measurable benefits when you train yourself to observe your own internal dialogue. In a surprisingly short period of time, you will have the tools to make your life as wonderful as you wish. You will be pleasantly surprised at how quickly you learn and adapt to the knowledge that you are the person who is responsible for your happiness. You will begin to recognise how flawed information or unrealistic expectations are major causes of dissatisfaction.

Unresolved issues act like daily irritants that breed dissatisfaction and block happiness. Most of us have an unconscious set of internal rules about how we and others should think, feel and behave. Our brains are programmed to believe that certain behaviours are desirable and others are undesirable; certain emotions are acceptable, others are unacceptable, and it's wrong to have feelings that fit into the unacceptable category.

Life will get so much better for you when you give

yourself credit for doing the best you knew how to do with the information you had at every stage of your life. Your programming, not you, put chocolate into the category of 'guilty pleasures'. Just as you have choices about whether you react to the food you eat with pleasure or guilt, you have choices about how you respond emotionally in every situation.

Whether you are aware of it or not, you have an emotional response to what your partner does or doesn't do. You are responsible for how you respond. You don't consciously stop to decide how you want to feel. It's as if a programmed reaction is triggered in you, and unconsciously, you have reacted before you could stop to think why you felt so pleased, happy and grateful or disappointed, angry and humiliated.

Alcoholism is a disease that no person chooses but the decision of an alcoholic to take the first drink is solely the responsibility of the person. It would be foolish and irresponsible to deny the emotional pain and distress of a person who is living with a partner who has an addiction to alcohol, drugs or gambling. There is no doubt that a partner's behaviour triggers a reaction, but it is also true that each person has a choice about how they react in every situation.

If you wish, you could look at past mistakes as opportunities for learning how to do better in the future. All of us have been in situations when we did not act as our best selves. If we had been thinking clearly and acted in a different way, it's likely that the outcome would have been very different. There is no good reason to hold on to regrets for something that exists in a memory, and not in present reality. If you behaved badly, did you try to make things right? Make reparation if that is possible and forgive yourself.

Your thoughts and memories of what happened in the past

are very real for you, but they are fantasies. The past and future exist only in your mind. You can entertain negative thoughts and distress yourself or you can free yourself from them. It's your choice. It may be true that the past and the future feel very real for you. Focus on either and they take you out of living life in the present moment.

You can only live life one moment at a time, which is why the spiritual masters teach that the present moment is never intolerable. Life becomes difficult if your body is in one location and your mind is elsewhere, remembering the past or catastrophising about the future. Where you focus your attention is a choice. When you decide to bring your attention to a new thought, the old ones will no longer exist. Surely this is standing in your own power!

6

THE MASKS WE WEAR AND THE ROLES WE PLAY

Owning our story can be hard but not nearly as difficult as spending our lives running from it.

BRENÉ BROWN

At a logical level you know that perfect people do not exist, but many of us secretly wish that we are wrong. We hold on to the illusion that a perfect partnership just might be a possibility. Perhaps a tiny little part wishes that we could be the happy couple that defies the odds.

In romantic stories, people live happily ever after. In real life, people need to communicate about their changing needs and wants to build an emotionally healthy partnership. If you want your partner to support you in the way you feel you need to be supported, you must be willing to be honest, to allow yourself to be vulnerable and frank about how you feel.

Honesty is the foundation of trust in a partnership and is a necessary component for intimacy. Say your emotional connection to your partner is not everything you want it to be. It may be because you lack the freedom to let your partner know when your feelings are hurt or your needs are not being met. To engage fully in an emotionally intimate relationship, you need to have trust in yourself as well as your partner. You need to have the confidence that you will feel safe if you allow yourself to be vulnerable with your partner.

It takes courage, effort and resilience to be who you are, to take off the mask you wear and to stop acting nicer than you feel. I'm confident you can adapt and cope with what life puts in your path. If you decide to be truly yourself, every relationship you have will get much better in a very short period of time.

You are the most important person in your relationship. You play many roles and wear many masks as you interact with your partner, family, friends and others. Imagine you are having a bad day and you choose to let your partner see you at your worst. Does the thought of allowing yourself to be so vulnerable make you feel insecure? Or can you honestly say that you feel confident that your partner has seen the best of you and the worst of you?

Couples who relate well are familiar with some of the strategies their partner uses when they want something. They can predict that their partner has an ulterior motive when he or she seems more co-operative or pleasant than usual. For example, he plays ultra-nice when he is hoping she will agree to go with him to a family gathering that he's afraid she won't enjoy. She has a knack of dropping hints about what he can do for her if she does what he wants.

Most of us recognise the strategies our partners use in this kind of quid pro quo manipulation. In this context, I am not talking about the persistent, excessive, over-the-top affection and flattery that a controlling partner might use. I invite clients to recognise what I refer to as 'WIIFM' which translates into 'what's in it for me?'. Ideally, what I call 'the art of healthy manipulation' ends up with enlightened self-interest. He gets something, she gets something, and they are both happy with the outcome.

In the book *Games People Play*, Eric Berne writes, 'We are rarely conscious of the games we play. But we keep playing them, even the destructive ones because we inherit them from childhood.'

Couples who come for relationship coaching will often say that they get on quite well much of the time but have issues they need help to resolve. The power to resolve issues lies with the people who created the problems in the first place. My coaching contract with clients is that I will use my coaching skills to empower them to help themselves. Partners have the solutions if they learn to work together amicably to solve their own problems. Most couples lack the necessary communication skills to deal effectively with conflict.

This is why coaching sessions often give people far better outcomes than they expected or hoped to achieve. When I agree to work with couples, I tell them, 'I will be honest with you and I expect you to be totally honest with me. I will give you the tools you need to empower you to build both your relationship and communication skills, and to use them well. I expect that in the process you will be able to figure out and understand why you could not do this alone.'

My belief is that I don't help clients. I put them on the path to helping themselves. If I, as a coach, believe that I can help someone, I'm labelling myself as an expert and doing a monumental disservice to my client. To deny a person the powerful learning experience of discovering they have the solution to their own problems is a travesty. I'm aware that many of my colleagues have different beliefs. I accept that they are right, but I am right too.

As a professionally trained Co-Active coach, my role when working with couples is to empower both people to communicate effectively. Partners need to have a conversation about how they set up their partnership. The clients who understand how they created a problem are better equipped to find a solution that will work for them both. Effective coaching empowers partners to quickly identify the underlying reasons for the frustrations and fights they have. I like to paraphrase the wise old saying, 'Tell me and I forget. Show me and I remember. Involve me and I understand how to live with an underlying sense of wholeness and wellbeing.'

Relationship coaching demands a level of respect and emotional honesty from the coach and the clients. Asking probing questions that expose dysfunctional patterns in how people relate involves careful word choice. People wear masks, play different roles and lie to their partners all the time. This is the plain, unvarnished truth.

Our day-to-day life presents what comedian Jerry Seinfeld calls 'must-lie situations' in which people lie precisely because they believe it is the right thing to do. Some couples who live together for a few years continue to behave romantically towards each other but if they marry, it changes how they relate. What co-habiting for a short period of time will not automatically do is alert you to your own expectations about what you want and need in a monogamous, enduring partnership.

Your needs will change over time and what feels good at one time in your life may not be at all satisfying at another. Some couples live together for many years without marrying but in every other way behave like a married couple. Marriage counsellors and coaching colleagues tell me that in their experience, couples in long-term partnerships are more likely than married couples to work through problems rather than ignore them.

What is undeniable is that people who want to impress a partner are on their best behaviour. They behave like model citizens: thoughtful, attentive and caring. Sadly, this cannot last because it is not the person's natural way of being. Reality will set in. The fantasy will end when illusions are shattered and cracks appear in the 'perfect' partnership.

Did you have expectations of living blissfully together? Or did you have expectations of how you and your partner would change after the first six months, two years or twenty years? Did you find that whatever expectations you had of living happily ever after were not met?

Who tells you that if your romantic illusions are shattered, you will probably fall slightly out of love? There is very little written about the in-between stages that every couple goes through when you love but don't like your partner. These are the times when it's important to look for the cracks, to look for what's broken and in need of fixing.

The Japanese have a beautiful practice called *kintsugi*. When an item of value is broken, they rejoin the broken fragments with lacquer and gold, leaving a gold seam where the cracks were. The symbolism of making a beautiful object out of something that might have been discarded is a powerful analogy for partners. The life lesson *kintsugi* teaches is when the cracks appear in a partnership and things appear to be falling apart, it's possible to put work into making what is imperfect into something potentially stronger and more beautiful.

Relationships go through numerous changes daily. You may be more aware of how your partner's moods change than of how your own feelings change your moods. Cracks begin to appear in a partnership when couples are not communicating. What made you and your partner happy at one time will change. Your sex life will suffer if you're frustrated or irritated as often as you are happy.

For some couples, small cracks in the relationship appear at about the two-year mark, for others serious cracks show around 'the seven-year itch' period. Only a tiny number of partners are as besotted twenty years into the relationship as they were when they fell in love.

People can't know what you don't tell them. Charlie started out married life with the expectation of staying in love. The honeymoon period of her marriage with Jack lasted almost two years and was amazing. At one time she would have found it impossible to imagine that her feelings would change or that she would ever fall out of love or be bored with her husband. She found it frustrating that Jack took her for granted and for her, the romance was ebbing in their relationship.

Neither of them was good at talking about their feelings. Jack sensed that something was not right when Charlie stopped initiating sex but when he asked her what was wrong, she told him, 'nothing'. Lack of satisfaction is a two-way process. Charlie's refusal to explain why she was frustrated by Jack's behaviour deprived him of the information he needed to try to put things right.

Jack worried about his sexual performance. He was worried about erectile dysfunction, which happened twice when he had too much alcohol to drink. Charlie told him it was just 'brewer's droop' and nothing to worry about. Her reassurance didn't stop him worrying, and this had an impact on their sex drive.

Finding the words to talk about their feelings, their needs and how they cope with their emotions is daunting for any couple. Negativity and tension between couples who are unable or unwilling to communicate honestly about their upset feelings begins as an 'embryo' that will grow and develop into 'the elephant in the room'.

Seemingly small issues that are easily dismissed as unimportant in the early stages of a relationship can build up into major sources of friction. Perhaps the first time you wanted to talk and your partner shut you out, you felt surprised. When it happened again, your feelings were upset and your partner's continued unwillingness to talk inflicted emotional pain every time it happened.

Silence, the refusal to talk, feels like a rejection. If you believe that your partner pushed you away, the emotional response is to feel hurt and you may experience a distance building between you. The lack of support and the feeling of being shut out are two of the most common complaints women have about partners who won't talk about feelings.

When issues that need to be addressed are ignored, they become a constant source of friction. Controlling behaviour, nagging, jealousy, emotional neglect, dishonesty, and lack of financial transparency are among the long list of complaints that unhappy partners bring up in their coaching sessions. Unresolved issues generate dissatisfaction, which discourages intimacy. When one partner is distressed by issues that the other ignores, anger and frustration (which are healthy emotions) can overshadow the belief that 'if my partner really loved me, I would not be ignored'.

In the same way that large oak trees grow from little acorns, repetitive unresolved issues between a couple can grow out of all proportion. If your expectations of your partner were not met and your illusions about how you believed your partner would treat you were shattered, I can guarantee that you started out with unrealistic expectations of being a couple. The old saying, 'anticipation is better than realisation' is so true.

Wrong information and unrealistic expectations are a

monumental obstacle to happiness. Much of what you believe about being happy with an intimate partner you learned from watching what your parents modelled in their couple relationship. It's important to be aware of how modelling may involve a lack of, as well as the presence of, good relationship skills.

As a child, you observed how your parents treated each other, how they showed affection, talked to each other, had fun, quarrelled and made up. Did you see them make up? Say you never saw your mum and dad fight, do you think it's because they were never angry with each other? If you did see your parents fight, what happened? Did they scream at each other, nag, name call, blame, criticise or hit out? Do you repeat what was modelled for you?

These are very personal questions that challenge you to look at your family of origin. The answers you give to the questions will play a major role in understanding and owning your own story. What is true for you is equally true for your partner. Your partner's beliefs about how men and women treat each other were well established before you even met and affect you in ways you have little knowledge of or control over.

Your expectations of being in a loving partnership are powerfully influenced by what you saw modelled for you, whether you were reared in a traditional two-parent family, or you had two mums or two dads, grew up in a lone parent family or one of your parents cheated and was unfaithful. If there was trauma in your family, what memories do you have about what happened?

Were you a happy or unhappy child? Among the issues unhappy children must cope with are an emotionally absent or neglectful parent. Some children who grow up in lone-parent families have wonderful childhoods, others don't. If you were brought up in a lone-parent family, was it because of parental separation, divorce or death?

If one of your parents died, how old were you? What do you remember? If this was your experience, how did the parent you lived with talk about the parent who died? If your parents were at war with each other, did one parent try to alienate you from the other?

Some of your early experiences of family life may be like your partner's. Many of them will be very different. All of us carry the unconsciously learned lessons of our upbringing in our heads. You have beliefs about how men and women treat each other, show affection, fight and make up, speak about problems, and share household tasks. All of these affect how you relate to your partner.

Your early experience in life will not be the same as your partner's, and because of those differences, you may be sensitive to issues that it may not occur to you to talk about. Did your mother treat you differently from the way your father did? Were you a daddy's girl or your mother's favourite? Did anyone in either family suffer from addiction or mental health issues?

You cannot change what you don't acknowledge. An obstacle that many clients have to overcome is the issues in their relationship that they are blind to but are a huge irritant to a partner who is silent about annoying habits, social skills deficits, lying, or irresponsible spending.

To communicate effectively, it is not enough to have a facility for words. You need the ability to focus, to hear and understand the words you listen to, and what is even more important, you need to be aware that the non-verbal signals like eye contact and body language communicate much more than any message conveyed in words.

The Masks we Wear and the Roles we Play

If you are a reader of women's magazines, you may have come across articles that say that married people live longer, have better health, earn more money, accumulate more wealth, feel more successful in their lives, enjoy more satisfying sexual relationships and have happier, more successful children. This may be true but is it also true that you will find research that disagrees with these articles and paints a less rosy picture of marital relationships.

When the levels of satisfaction in a partnership diminish and the sense of trust and emotional connection deteriorate, fractious partners can become bitter and hostile. Some who have a love/hate relationship have mixed feelings about what to do. The decision about whether to stay in or leave a miserable and unhappy relationship is complex and not one to be taken lightly.

It's easy to notice dysfunctional patterns in other people's relationships and much harder to see the same patterns in your own or your partner's actions. You won't necessarily repeat your parents' experience but if you want a very different kind of relationship from the one your parents had, you need to take a long, hard, honest look at what you're thinking and what you're feeling. Trying to understand why you feel and act the way you do is well worth your while.

Many people wrongly believe that if they could only change their partner's behaviour, they would feel calmer and happier. You know that you can't control your partner. It is useless to attempt to change him or her. So, if you are dissatisfied and less than happy, you can drop any expectation you have of changing your partner or yourself.

'People cannot change their basic essence even if they try, and it is futile to demand that they do so,' said Andrew Christensen, who for more than twenty years worked with hundreds of couples in therapy. He illustrated how we can be annoyed by the same traits that initially attracted us with a *Cathy* cartoon. Cathy's mother says to her: 'When you met Irving, you raved about his ambition. When you broke up, you called him a 'self-absorbed workaholic'. When you met Alex, you gushed about his free spirit. When you broke up, he was 'directionless and immature'.'

Christensen suggests that more of the change we seek in our relationships is gradual change in everyday behaviour: 'Do more of the housework; spend more time with the kids; don't be so critical; pay more attention when I talk to you; be more ambitious at work; put more energy into our relationship.'

There is no such thing as a perfect partnership. People who believe that true love should require no effort, who think that if your partner truly loves you, you will live harmoniously for the rest of your lives, are delusional. Happiness in a relationship does not depend on harmony. Neither does it depend on how your partner or spouse treats you. Believe it or not, your happiness depends on you, on your beliefs, actions and attitudes.

What you believe to be true becomes true for you. A person who believes their partner has the power to make them feel happy has given that person control over their emotions. There is no denying that if you believe that someone can make you feel happy, you must accept that they can also make you feel sad. You, and not your partner, are in control of what you are thinking.

Your partner's actions may trigger positive or negative feelings in you, but how you feel emotionally is your personal response to how you think. If you decide to put up and shut up, that decision to 'play nice' is an impediment that blocks a real emotional connection with your partner.

Do you recall how amazing you felt when you were first

with your partner? Among other emotions, you probably felt beautiful, sexy, funny, clever. Those qualities were already in you but were not available to you until you fell in love. Something is freed when you fall in love that allows you to dip into your wellsprings of untapped potential, and you have the confidence to act as your best self.

At our core, we all need to feel loved and lovable and it is a most wonderful experience while it lasts. Unfortunately, the 'in love' stages in partnerships are transient. It is surprising how quickly partners begin to take each other for granted. People who have been together for years can know intellectually that their partner loves them but feel like they are in a loveless relationship.

Women are more likely than men to articulate the desire to feel loved, to feel special, and have their partners acknowledge their presence when they enter a room. There is a world of difference between intellectually knowing that you are loved and emotionally feeling loved.

Your partner cannot give you the love you need to give yourself. Gandhi is credited with saying, 'Be the change you want to see in the world.' You cannot fix a problem until you know what the problem is. An issue for people who have broken up with a partner or partners in the past is that when they walk away from a bad relationship, they carry baggage with them that has the potential to contaminate a new relationship.

Some people who are unhappy and dissatisfied have very little insight into what is wrong in their relationship. They want something more or different but they are unable to say what specifically they desire. So, if you want a happier relationship, it's up to you to figure out how to have an emotionally healthy relationship with yourself first.

Many of your beliefs about happy couple partnerships

come from what you saw modelled by your parents. Perhaps you decided not to behave like your parents but find yourself doing and saying things that you swore you would never do. Or you may have decided to do the opposite and be as different from your parents as you could be.

Whether you're aware of it or not, many of the expectations you have of how you want your partner to treat you will have their origins in what you saw modelled as a child. Other expectations will be powerfully affected by media influences, by the Hollywood images of romance that everybody knows are fictional but also seem desirable.

In her book, *Flourishing*, psychologist Maureen Gaffney writes, 'When you have to deal with challenges of one kind or another all the time, you only thrive when you own the challenge in a personal way. A crisis may be brewing for a long time or it may come as a bolt from the blue. It may take time for you to fully appreciate what is happening. But there is always a particular moment when you decide to take it on and to see it through.' Make this your moment to own the challenge in a personal way, take it on and see it through.

I have worked with many clients who came for couple coaching when they reached that 'moment of change'. Some clients harboured the belief that their unhappiness was caused by their partner and their lives would improve if the other person would shape up (meet their expectations) and act more responsibly. The myth that it's up to your partner to make your life better is widely believed. Relationships are transformed when that myth is shattered and each partner learns to take personal responsibility.

People are usually very definite about what they don't want and much less clear about what will give them the feelings they believe they will enjoy when they feel happy, content and fulfilled with a partner. 'How do you know you are happy?' is a powerful coaching question and is not an easy one to answer. Even people who are emotionally aware find it a difficult question because words are inadequate to describe an emotion. Do you have realistic expectations if you cannot name the criteria for how you measure happiness?

It is likely that your criteria for happiness changes as often as you change your mind. What makes you deliriously happy at one time can leave you feeling cold at another. You're bound to feel unfulfilled and dissatisfied if you complain that the spark has gone out of your relationship. Is it possible that the issues in your partnership have less to do with your partner and more to do with your own insecurities or a lack of willingness to be honest with yourself and with your partner?

One small change in the language you use can make the difference that makes a difference. Words have power. The reaction to a sentence that begins with the word 'you' will elicit a different response to one that starts with 'I feel'. 'You' is frequently heard as a complaint and interpreted as assigning blame. If I tell my partner, 'I felt angry when you were late', I take ownership of how I feel. The statement, 'You made me angry' is not true but it has the potential to sour a relationship if it sounds like an accusation, especially if your partner's belief is, 'I have done nothing wrong'.

Your relationship is as good as your communication. Your communication is as good as your ability to listen and that listening starts with paying attention to what you say to yourself. I have seen many relationships blossom when partners realised that they were jointly responsible for the state of their relationship and agreed to make small changes in how they communicated.

Logically, you know that your partner cannot make you feel happy, sad or miserable unless you unwittingly gave them the power to do so. Intellectually, you may accept that you are responsible for how you feel. Even when you know this, you may find that a part of you still blames your partner for triggering negative emotions in you.

There is nothing unusual in having a part of you that appears to conflict with other parts. If you ask, 'What is your positive intention for blaming?' be open to hear the answer. It might be to avoid taking responsibility. It could be a fear of owning an uncomfortable truth that affects how you think of yourself. Or it could be something very different.

Self-acceptance can be hard. People don't want to live with the emotional distress that we are conditioned to avoid. Loving and accepting yourself unconditionally is difficult because it means living authentically. Removing the social masks, dropping the fantasy narratives, and taking full responsibility for your thoughts and feelings will not happen overnight. Let it happen in incremental stages as you persevere with the goals you set for yourself.

7

HOME TRUTHS

But I know, somehow, that only when it is dark enough can you see the stars.

MARTIN LUTHER KING JR

Is it logical to blame or judge a partner negatively if needs that were never voiced are not met? At one level, you know that it's not your partner's role in life to live up to your expectations or demands. Knowing this will not eliminate the feelings of hurt you experience when you are upset with your partner for failing to meet your needs. That's just being human.

It's challenging and difficult to accept that you have the quality of relationship you unconsciously colluded with your partner in creating. If you do not know what you want yourself, isn't it unrealistic to expect your partner to anticipate what you want, desire and expect?

To believe that someone's behaviour hurt you is understandable. When one person does not seem to notice or care that their partner is anxious, worried or upset, the emotional impact can feel like an open wound. It would be unwise to assume that if only the two of you had better communication, if you could talk to each other calmly about your feelings, your partner would be able to give you the support and the understanding you crave.

Your efforts to make anyone understand the depth of your emotional pain, distress and worry are bound to fail. You may believe that if your partner truly loved you, they would treat you differently. Wrong again. Your upset is not about your partner, even though it may feel that way. It is about you. Your emotional pain comes from what you believe, what you tolerate and what you excuse. This may be hard to accept, but it is true.

The inner turmoil experienced by someone who loves a partner who behaves in ways that triggers them to react with angry and frustrated feelings is stressful. It's helpful to have criteria for knowing your stress levels. When you are stressed, do you have the freedom to be honest with your partner – no white lies, no massaging the truth, no censoring or holding back?

What stops you from expressing yourself freely and with confidence is you. Whether you are aware of your motivation for expressing or hiding your feelings, the emotions you bury or deny affect you, often very deeply. I have no doubt that you have good reasons for what you do and don't do.

I understand if you rationalise that the reason you don't confront problem issues is you're too busy to do anything right now. Maybe you tried in the past and your partner went silent and shut you out. Or maybe your partner is unaware of your distress. When unacceptable behaviour is overlooked, excused or tolerated, a partner can claim ignorance and ask, 'How could I have known?'

You need to look at what is going on in your partnership if you remain silent about the times you don't feel loved or feel offended when your partner is disrespectful to you. Tears can be a genuine outpouring of grief but they can also be used to manipulate and control. Sobbing can be faked. A common deflection during difficult conversations is for one partner to burst into tears and get so emotionally distressed that it shuts down any hope of having a rational conversation.

When I work with a client who genuinely believes that it

is their partner who is the problem, I know that what I call the black-and-white thinking of 'I'm right and you're wrong' is at play. Our brains are programmed to find someone to blame when our feelings are hurt. If a toddler who is learning to walk bangs off a chair and cries, the reaction of the adults in the room is to smack the chair. A child who hears, 'bold chair hurt you' gets the message that when you feel hurt, someone or something out there is to blame.

You may believe that your wisest option is to ignore what you feel in the hope that the relationship will get better. It won't. There comes a time when, for your own wellbeing, you need a wake-up call. You need to get real and take the rose-tinted spectacles off and face some painful truths about yourself and your partner.

We all have flaws and failings. It's part of the human condition. Let's say Tony has many good qualities. When his relationship with Jane is good, it's very good. Jane hates that her kind and loving partner tells lies, betrays her confidences and says mean and angry things that wound her deeply. When things between Tony and Jane are bad, they are very bad.

Jane's way of dealing with these problem issues is to minimise her partner's ill treatment of her. She tells family members that Tony didn't really mean what he said. Tony has little incentive to change because Jane consistently overlooks and excuses behaviour that he is ashamed of himself. Passive partners, who make excuses or placate a partner, do themselves no favours.

It takes honesty and courage to examine how you colluded with your partner to build the partnership you have today. No matter what is going on in your life, you can, if you wish, make time for reflection. See if there is something going on in you that makes you fear or wish to avoid bringing this up in a conversation. Find out why you say you are too busy to take time to reflect on where the real problem lies.

What does it say about your self-care if you fail to make yourself a priority? Your emotional state is important because expressing your feelings is an essential component of intimacy with a partner. Finding the appropriate words to say how you feel is a huge challenge. Self-revelation makes us vulnerable. A valid fear may be that a partner might dismiss your feelings or refuse to listen or say you shouldn't have those feelings. The person who has a bullying partner who gets angry and is verbally or physically abusive may feel too afraid to speak up.

The best predictor of future behaviour is past behaviour. Making the decision to be really honest and tell it like it is takes a lot of courage and determination. However, it is essential if you want to be happy and have peace of mind. A useful image that is helpful for understanding how you are affected by unexpressed feelings is to imagine an elastic band that is stretched to its limits. When enough tension builds up, the elastic band will snap.

The longer you hold on to your unexpressed feelings, the more the tension will grow between you and your partner. The longer you refuse to take action, the more the stress builds until eventually the tension becomes too much and something snaps. When that happens, one or both of you is bound to get hurt.

I believe about eighty per cent of the decisions we make are motivated by fear, not desire. You cannot have an intact sense of self-worth if you decide to keep the peace at all costs. Are you wary of confrontation, scared of retaliation, fearful of the consequences if you open 'a can of worms'?

Any decision you make that is based in fear steals your

freedom to be who you are. If you feel coerced into meeting a real or imagined demand, and you do the expected thing and conform, you are not free. People resent the perceived demand to do what is expected, even when it is their own expectations of themselves. If you say, 'I should, must, ought or have to', you give yourself no choice. Please recognise how feeling disempowered leaks self-confidence and diminishes self-worth.

To be in a relationship where you feel sad and miserable more often than you feel happy and secure is not an emotionally healthy place for anyone to be. Some of the logical reasons that people use to convince themselves to stay with a partner are: you have no place to go; you don't have the financial means to parent alone; you don't want to be on your own; you don't want to uproot your children; it is better to live with the hope that things can and will get better than give up on the relationship.

Later, I will ask you to look at what is good about the relationship you have with your partner and what is wrong with the relationship you have with yourself. As you become more self-aware and take more responsibility for your own happiness, you may find that beliefs you held all your adult life no longer serve you well.

Are you willing to make the effort necessary to feel emotionally healthy, happy, and content with life? A good start is to love and accept yourself exactly as you are, not as you would like to be. Fix yourself before you even begin to think of how to fix your partnership. Are you gentle, tolerant and compassionate with yourself? If your answer is 'no', you lack the resources to be gentle, tolerant and empathetic with your partner. Logic tells us that you cannot give to your partner what you do not have for yourself.

Reflect on how you manage your life and emotions. What

do you say to yourself about yourself? Pay close attention to the tone of your own internal dialogue. Listen out for negative self-talk – the things you say about yourself that you would be horrified to say in public about anyone else. Do you need to speak more kindly and gently? Is your voice soft or harsh? Do you sound loving, compassionate and tolerant or are there critical judgements that are hurtful and unkind?

I have worked with clients who were in shock when they became aware of how often they were intolerant, judgemental and disrespectful about themselves. Giving yourself time for reflection mirrors the love, value and appreciation you give to yourself. Do you have clarity about what upsets you and why? Where do you get triggered? Take this as an opportunity to go inside and figure out where the upset is coming from. Discover how your internal dialogue upsets you.

A hard question is, 'Can you be in an emotionally healthy partnership if you are "walking on eggshells" trying to keep your partner sweet?' You do not have an equal partnership if you make excuses for your partner's words or actions. Verbal abuse and nasty jokes damage partnerships. Abuse of any kind should never be tolerated. It's important to seek help as early as possible if a partner is abusive or you feel threatened. If you have a fear or an intuition that a partner may become violent, please heed the warning.

It's challenging for a client to admit that they have allowed themselves to be a victim of any kind of abuse. A combination of pride and shame will motivate a person who feels emotionally or physically unsafe to conceal how they are mistreated. Practical issues such as being financially dependent or the fear of creating a scandal that would affect family members are often behind the decision to stay in an unsafe partnership.

Many of us were programmed to make the needs of others more important than our own. I often ask clients, 'For what purpose do you put your own needs last or ignore them completely?' Is it because of your programming? Or is it because it meets some of your needs and in that sense, in a perverse way, it works for you?

You learned to seek parental approval at a very early age. If you were praised when you did nice things for others, you enjoyed the appreciation and felt validated. If you put your own needs first, you were called 'selfish'. The need for approval is part of the motivation when we make the needs of others more important than our own needs.

The bible gives excellent advice about what I call 'healthy selfishness'. 'Love God and love your partner as yourself'. My lay person's interpretation of this is to give your own needs the same importance as you give to your partner's needs. This is not selfish and so there is no reason to have guilty feelings for taking care of you.

Don't be surprised if your programmed brain generates uncomfortable thoughts. Are you acting selfishly if you make yourself a priority? Answer either 'yes' or 'no'. If you answered 'yes', your programmed brain needs an update. What is selfish is to sacrifice your own needs and blame your partner.

Any sacrifices you make to keep the peace, or feel good about yourself, are your sole responsibility. If you feel taken for granted, not appreciated and valued for all you do for your partner, it is highly likely that you have a limited understanding of how the values and beliefs you espouse block your happiness.

Your personal values and beliefs are important because they are a central part of who you are. Values are the rules we live by and you may discover that what you think of as 'your values' are inherited and not yours. If honesty is one of your personal values and you tell lies, you will experience inner turmoil. By breaching your own rules, you violate trust, feel untrustworthy and generate internal conflict.

If love and trust are two of your values, you may believe that you are a loving and trustworthy person. Love and trust are like two sides of the same coin. Without trust, you cannot be in an authentically loving partnership.

Let's check out the belief that you are trustworthy:

- Do you trust yourself to always do what you say you will do?
- Do you always keep your promises?
- Is there a gap between what you say you believe and what you actually believe?

It may be true that most of the time you believe you can be depended on to do what you say you will do. Usually you keep your promises, but there are times when you don't for very valid reasons. On occasion, you must prioritise because you have competing commitments. Making a different commitment a priority does not necessarily make you a bad person. It does suggest that when you fail to do what you intended and promised to do, you have let both yourself and the other person down.

What would be different in your life if you set a goal of being authentic? How would you feel about yourself if you made the decision to always behave congruently with your values and beliefs? There is no doubt that this would be a challenge, but you are more than capable of achieving any realistic goal you set for yourself.

In the process, you may have to change some habits, challenge wrong beliefs and adapt to changes that will at times be difficult. A mantra that many of my clients have found helpful is: 'I can do this. I will do this. I will not stop myself from doing this.'

Self-belief is a wonderful resource. In my experience of coaching clients who seek to be authentically themselves, there are three issues that need to be worked on:

- Discover who you are.
- Improve your communication skills.
- Get real and drop your unrealistic expectations.

One of the labels that people put on the emotion they feel when they experience what they describe as a positive response is happiness. You are one hundred per cent responsible for reaching your own goal so for now, let's focus totally on your personal quest for happiness.

Most of us have a belief that when we achieve an outcome we desire, we'll experience happiness. No two people experience an emotion in the same way. What you believe makes for happiness in you is not consistent. Coffee tasted disgusting to you when you were a child. As an adult, it may be your favourite beverage, a stimulant you believe you cannot do without.

What you tell yourself becomes true for you. Words like joy, fulfilment, happiness and satisfaction can be interchangeable because there is no one word to accurately describe how you react physically to what you see and hear and smell and taste and touch. You may not be aware that you have a way of labelling or coding your different emotions.

How do you tell the difference between any two emotions? Do you experience joy and happiness, fear and excitement, sadness or grief in the same ways? If you say they are not identical and some are more intense than others, how do you know this?

Most people can tell if they are in a good or bad mood, but not everyone. I often ask a client to select two feelings (for example, anger and happiness) and explain how they know which is which. Everybody knows that there is a difference. To explain how they code the difference is challenging.

Many clients describe body language; for anger, it may be clenched fists or for happiness, it could be smiling. That is the reaction or response to the feeling but not the answer to 'how do you know which is which?' Only a small number can identify and give a word for the physical sensations they experience and label as a specific emotion.

When an emotion is experienced, it sets off a series of impulses in your body and in your brain, which leads to specific psychological effects. Whether you feel happy or sad, you experience immediate changes in your body, and in your autonomic nervous system.

With a pleasant emotion, the heartbeat increases, the breathing becomes faster, and the whole body feels warmer or lighter. With a so-called 'negative emotion', the feelings can be unpleasant or uncomfortable. Painful feelings, if they are intense, can almost take the breath away. The muscles tense, the chest tightens, which constricts breathing, crying may be uncontrollable and heart palpitations can occur.

People tend to think of excitement as a positive emotion and fear as a negative feeling before they engage in the work of emotional awareness. For many people, the physical sensations for these feelings are so similar that I suggest they look on 'FEAR' as a 'false expectation appearing real' and on 'excitement' as 'feeling excited and ready'.

What is your motivation when you do something that you would prefer not to do? Are you seeking love, needing approval, looking for appreciation, or trying to avoid conflict? Clients who believe they need to control what they do to avoid conflict live with a perceived threat. This puts them constantly on the alert, which is stressful.

Very few people take the time to be fully aware of why they do what they do and why they make the decisions they make. Would it make a difference to how you feel about yourself if you had the integrity to be fully yourself and made your needs as important as your partner's needs? The answers to the following questions may reveal obstacles that get in the way of doing this:

- Do you say 'yes' when you want to say 'no'?
- Do you make your partner's needs more important than your own?
- Do you treat your partner better than you treat yourself?

What is it about your belief system that allows you to bury your feelings? If you act the role of an agreeable, co-operative partner and avoid asking for your needs to be met, you are not being fair to your partner. Hiding negative feelings serves no good purpose.

I have no doubt that you have a positive reason when you put your partner's needs first. Please know that your actions mirror the beliefs and values you hold. Given your emotional state, your education, life experience and family background, you always do the very best that you can, with the resources you have.

When you look back with the benefit of hindsight, you have knowledge of the outcome of the actions you took. However, if you were back in any situation from the past with only the information you had at the time, you could only make the decisions you made back then.

Tolerance and patience are not virtues if they are used as an excuse for condoning unacceptable or inappropriate behaviour. No one would deny that the person who says one thing and means another is untrustworthy. In all honesty, you and I cannot deny that in multiple situations throughout our lives, we told lies. That is a fact and no excuse is necessary. Being untrustworthy does not make you a bad person. It's simply part of the human condition.

Saying 'yes' when you really want to say 'no' is counter-productive and affects your personal sense of integrity. People-pleasers who act nicer than they feel will never really feel secure with their partner because they only show their good side. The fear of what might happen if your partner really knew who you are is a monumental obstacle to true intimacy.

Barely noticed negative feelings that are suppressed do not disappear. Buried feelings put a strain on a relationship. What is not expressed is suppressed, and over time has the potential to breed insecurity and damage trust. What hardly anyone teaches you is that you cannot have an emotionally healthy relationship with a partner until you know who you are and you have the freedom to be authentically yourself.

We say we value the truth and we give credence to the belief that it is wrong to lie. Yet most of us rationalise that lying in certain circumstances is acceptable. If kindness is one of your values, you may believe that the right thing to do is to prioritise being kind over being honest. At the surface level, massaging the truth to make it more palatable may appear to be an act of kindness, but I question this.

When there is a lot of information competing for our attention, our brains must be selective. To prevent us from being overwhelmed by too much information, the brain has the capacity to rapidly switch back and forth between important and unimportant things. Selective attention is the term used when we focus on things that matter to us and ignore unimportant things. When we pay attention to one thing, it affects how we see other things.

Cognitive psychologist David Simons became famous for investigating what he called sustained perceptual or inattentional blindness. He produced a video of two teams of three people. One team wore white shirts and the other wore black shirts. The six players filled much of the video screen. Their facial features were close enough so as to be seen clearly. Each team had their own ball, which they bounced or threw to their own team members.

People who watched the video were asked to count how many times the people with the white shirts threw the ball back and forth to one another. After a few minutes, the viewers were asked to report the number of passes and most correctly answered fifteen. Then the viewers were asked, 'Did you see the gorilla?' This wasn't a joke.

The second time people were told to watch the video without counting. Sure enough, there was a man in a gorilla suit, as large as life. He walked right into the middle of the game for a few seconds. He stopped and beat his chest in the manner of stereotyped gorillas everywhere. The people who focused their attention on the game missed the gorilla.

When you focus your attention on one thing, you will often miss others that may be significant. In another study, Simons showed participants a video of someone being served at a counter. The server bent down to retrieve something and stood back up. Most of the participants did not notice that a different person stood up in the server's place. There was a high probability that the change of person was not detected even when the gender or race of the person was switched.

The world you live in is defined by your own perceptions. You do not consciously decide to focus on what you don't want in a relationship. However, if there are daily irritants that feel like the 'pebble in the shoe', you're more likely to be focused on the negative than on the positive. What you choose to overlook or ignore will often fade into the background.

So much unnecessary misery and unhappiness are unintentionally caused by a failure to communicate honestly and with integrity. The assumption that everyone tells lies is so widespread that hardly anyone stops to question why people don't tell the truth. It's probable that you learned to condone white lies and censor the truth before you went to school.

I never overlook a client's positive intention in wanting to spare a partner's feelings nor do I ignore the elements of control and judgement involved. To assume that a partner might not cope shows a lack of trust and respect for the ability of the other to resolve problems and deal with issues. Behind the decision to withhold information, there are usually elements of vulnerability, self-preservation and control.

Withholding information may deprive a partner of valuable facts that affect decision-making. At a surface level, it may appear to be the best option, but you cannot know this for a fact. Some people make what they believe are informed decisions when they decide how much of the truth their partner can handle. Censoring the information you share is lying by omission, which can do irreparable damage. The negative consequences when a partner is proved to be untrustworthy, either found to be lying or hiding the truth, will have a long-term, negative impact on a partnership.

Trust can be rebuilt over time but it is a slow and arduous process. You cannot change what you don't acknowledge. Misguided beliefs and wrong information may have been the motivation for past actions you feel guilty about and regret now. You cannot change what happened in the past, so don't torture yourself with guilty feelings about past situations.

The best advice you will hear about how to let go of guilt about past mistakes comes from poet and philosopher Maya Angelou: 'Do the best you can until you know better. Then, when you know better, do better.'

8

You are Not your Thoughts

Progress is impossible without change, and those who cannot change their minds cannot change anything.

GEORGE BERNARD SHAW

What is the response in you when you hear the word 'ego'? Do you think of the ego as the self? Do you have a sense that the word refers to who you are as a person? Or do you conjure up an image of someone you think of as an arrogant person who is full of him or herself?

'Ego' is the Latin word for 'I' and it came into psychology mostly through the work of Sigmund Freud. It begins to develop during the first three years of a child's life. A practical way for you to think of ego is to look at how it relates to your identity, your sense of awareness, your consciousness with your physical body, emotions and thoughts.

I have a great deal of sympathy for arrogant people who demand to be the centre of attention. People who appear to have big egos are usually insecure. Their way of concealing their sense of inadequacy is to act as if they are better than everyone else. Do you think that egotistical people would need to demonstrate a conflated sense of superiority if they truly loved themselves and had a healthy sense of self-worth and self-confidence?

Psychologists tell us that an overinflated ego is really a protective measure. It serves as a shield to avoid feeling vulnerable. I don't have the language to describe or explain what specifically 'ego' is. It is not, as some people believe, one's true

You are Not your Thoughts

self. It's an idea we have about who we are and this idea is based mostly on our perceptions, which mostly come from other people's opinions.

From the moment of birth, we are bombarded with messages about the sort of person others think we are. Psychologists suggest that the ego is always craving attention because it comes from a place of fear; fear of not being admired, fear of losing power, fear of not being liked, or fear of making a mistake. Overcoming the ego and releasing fear to come to the place where you have confidence in your own ability to deal with life's challenges involves hard work, self-awareness and emotional intelligence.

Christine came for life coaching because she was worried about herself. She was happily married for twenty-three years and had two teenage children who were great kids. Eighteen months earlier, she was diagnosed with breast cancer. The cancer was detected early and after chemotherapy and radiation treatment she made a good recovery.

This changed her outlook on life. She found it also changed her attitude to her family. Life had gone back to normal for them but not for her. She had been through a huge trauma. Her life had been turned upside down but her family ignored this. She had mixed feelings about the demands they made on her before she felt like she was almost back to herself.

She was a lovely person who felt guilty about explaining how disappointed and terribly resentful she felt towards her husband and children. While she was undergoing treatment, they were wonderfully caring. In one sense, she liked that they had gone back to taking her for granted. At another level, she resented it so much that she was worried that the stress from her negative feelings could bring the cancer back.

From a coaching perspective, there was nothing wrong

with Christine's response to her changed circumstances. How she reacted to her family's demands on her was appropriate. A patient recovering from treatment after a life-challenging illness will go through a process of grieving for the life and family relationships they had before they were diagnosed.

Relationships change when a family member is treated for cancer. Christine felt closer to her family when she was ill. While she was undergoing treatment, they were wonderful but once she was in remission, they acted differently. They were less caring and left her to pick up after them as they went about their normal activities.

My intuition was that she was still recovering emotionally and physically and she didn't want her life to go back to how it was before her illness. I have no doubt that she would have felt reassured if I said all this but I chose not to deprive her of the powerful life lessons she would discover with experiential understanding.

By asking powerful coaching questions that invite clients to reflect at a deeper level than they thought possible, people gain insights that offer them a clear, accurate and sometimes sudden understanding of where their issues lie. This is where the solution to their problems is found and the necessary steps to achieving a goal emerge.

Some clients who come for coaching want things to be different but when asked about what specifically they want, they simply don't know. Questions I often ask are:

- What do you want to gain from coaching?
- What do you want to change?
- What do you do for fun?

When I asked Christine these questions she answered, 'I don't know' to the first question, 'What do you want to gain from coaching?' Then she apologised for not having an answer. Her reply to the second question, 'What do you want to change?' was 'I don't know. It's not something I think about.' She was taken aback by my response when I asked, 'What do you do for fun?' She blurted out, 'I no longer have fun in my life.' I said, 'Isn't that beautiful? Not knowing is a great place to start our work together.'

The coaching relationship is custom tailored to the communication approach that will work best for each client. Most people who seek the services of a coach have a lack of balance in one or more areas of their lives. At the core, they need to have a good life/family/work balance that honours their values.

The well-groomed, energetic person who arrives early carrying a briefcase will benefit from a different approach to the tired-looking client who sits slumped in a chair. No two people present in coaching with the same agenda. The details of their presenting issues will vary but the desire to feel happier and live more fully usually emerges from the wheel of life exercise.

The client is always in control of the coaching relationship and is ultimately responsible for the changes they make in their lives. The coach and client are active collaborators in an effective coaching relationship.

Christine loved the fact that the client sets the agenda and the coaching relationship is entirely focused on getting the results she desires. As an intelligent, self-aware woman, Christine liked the idea of working issues out for herself in a safe environment with a coach who would hold the agenda she brought to each coaching session.

Most clients appear uncomfortable when they don't have answers until I explain about 'the gremlin'. Everyone has a powerful internal sabotaging voice that sets them up for failure. Negative statements such as 'you don't have the answers', 'you shouldn't feel the way you do', and 'you should feel guilty about how you feel' are familiar to most of us. With the client's permission, I challenge these untruths, which I invite clients to think of as 'the ugly lies'.

Some clients expect a readymade solution to the issues they bring to coaching. Others expect to be coached by someone who has more experience or expertise in dealing with their issues. This is mentoring, not coaching. The skill of the coach is to ask the questions that allow the client to go inside to discover their strengths and limitations and work towards their goals or desired outcomes.

During this process, a client will probably become aware of limiting beliefs. They will come face to face with what they fear, and ideally will learn how to confront the ways they hold themselves back and stop themselves from achieving. These are some of the obstacles that clients need to overcome on their journey to becoming their best selves.

How do you respond to a person who apologises when they have done nothing wrong? The habit of saying 'sorry' is a self-defence mechanism that shows vulnerability. A client's fear of being judged will stop them from engaging honestly in challenging conversations about sensitive and difficult topics.

When the coach and client have rapport, it gives the coach the freedom to engage with curiosity, energy, creativity, interest and honesty in the sessions. I want the coaching environment for every client to feel safe. Rapport is essential to support and challenge a client, to take the risk of stepping out of their comfort zone; and to find the courage to engage in an honest and in-depth examination of their decision-making.

A coaching conversation is different from all other conversations. It has two purposes: to empower action and learning in a safe environment and to allow the client to grow, develop, and feel empowered to keep going when they experience a setback. The support when a coach shows confidence that a person can pick themselves up from a fall and recover energises clients to stay motivated and on track.

People have different levels of self-awareness. Some clients understand how their thoughts influence the moods they experience. I feel shocked by how many don't. Clients who previously had counselling tend to be attuned to how environmental experiences powerfully shape their beliefs, emotional reactions and actions.

Most clients are creatures of habit. They repeat the same behaviours over and over again. For example, take someone who finds it easier to give in than to disagree. The person is unlikely to have any awareness of the thought that guides their silent behaviour because putting up and shutting up has become automatic, a habitual response.

A type of thinking that influences mood and behaviour is what we call 'automatic thoughts', the words and images that constantly pop into a person's mind during the day as they are doing things to which they react automatically. When I coach clients who say they are taken for granted and they complain that they are frustrated because a partner fails to appreciate them, I almost always get a shocked reaction when I tell them, 'How wonderful that you're aware of that response in you. That's beautiful because frustration is an opportunity for learning. I know this is hard but I want you to think of frustration as a gift, maybe an unwanted gift, which your partner gives you to empower you to see where you need to grow.'

Parents who bring family issues to coaching will often have complaints about having to go upstairs to collect dirty dishes teenage children leave in their bedrooms. Telling yourself that you must do something you don't like doing is stressful. When the client checks out the accuracy of a statement such as 'I have to collect the dishes' they find no one is forcing them. It's a self-generated stress because of a flawed belief.

The first time a client is invited to check out the accuracy of a belief is always significant. Learning that one can make different choices comes at a price. Whenever you gain something in one area of your life, there is always the possibility that you or someone else will lose something in a different area.

Something I have learned over many years working with clients is that issues that present as minor irritants in the beginning frequently have deep roots. By offering clients a different way of looking and thinking about something they take for granted, their perceptions change. It's challenging to think of any negative feeling as a gift, but an unwanted, uncomfortable experience can shine a spotlight on where there is a need for growth.

If you examine the decisions you make and look at them from a different perspective, you will probably gain insights into what motivated you to take or not take action. Self-preservation is a powerful motivator. It's a shock to learn how frequently decisions are motivated by fear; fear of not being liked, fear of losing power, fear of conflict, fear of making a mistake, fear of retaliation, fear of letting oneself down.

Some people say, 'I'm shy. I could never speak in public. I couldn't do that.' Shy people speak in public all the time. They learn to overcome their fear by altering their internal dialogue from 'I can't' to 'I can'. I cannot emphasise enough how much attitude determines success and failure. The tragedy when you tell yourself, 'I couldn't do that' is that you deny yourself an opportunity. How can you know what you can achieve if you stop yourself with negative expectations?

The two words 'I can't' are more usually motivated by the fear of failure than by logical reasons that stand up to scrutiny. Overcome your fear by tagging on the word 'yet' and you may discover endless possibilities. Clients discover that if they take the right class, read the right book, or go to an effective life coach, they can achieve more than they ever thought possible.

Each one of us interacts with many different people over the course of our lives. You can probably name the people who bring out the best in you. Occasionally, we come across people who bring out the worst in us, even though we may not be able to figure out why they trigger us. If you want to discover how you are triggered, take a moment to focus on your contact with the person in your life who brings out the worst in you. Recall the event as if you were rewinding a video in slow motion. Work back from your reaction frame by frame. What were you aware of the second before you reacted?

It could be anything – a gesture, a tone of voice, the perfume or aftershave the person wore. Check if the person reminds you of someone or something from your past. It's not uncommon for a memory of a previous upsetting experience to be unconsciously projected onto someone in the present. Hold yourself accountable for your actions and reactions. Reactions and beliefs are interconnected.

If you have limiting beliefs that come from a fear of failure or of not measuring up to expectations, the fear will limit your ability to dip into your wellsprings of untapped potential. It would be a tragedy if you never discover the hidden gifts, talents and resources you have to achieve what you desire. Why would you allow the fear that you might not succeed prevent you finding out what you can accomplish? Why would you allow a person you have issues with live rent-free in your head?

Hardly anyone is conscious of how they learned to live up to other people's expectations. When you examine what motivates you to behave as you do, you may discover how you came to internalise the expectations others have of you. Some people are blessed with the support of a mentor who recognises the abilities they have. Others fail to recognise their own gifts and talents until they find the connections between how they think and feel, and discover what motivated them to act. Making the connection between thoughts, moods, environment and motivation has the potential to lead to profound changes in how we go after what we want.

Words have power and one's internal dialogue has the potential to become a self-fulfilling prophecy. The impact that thoughts and beliefs have on our health are well documented. Olympic athletes are coached to imagine in detail their performance in an event. Research shows that athletes who do this kind of vivid imagining actually experience small muscle contractions that reflect the bigger muscle movements they make in an actual performance.

Beliefs are thought processes based on knowledge, perceptions and life experiences. What you believe about yourself powerfully affects your emotions, behaviour and physiological reactions. For example, if you are standing in a queue for a taxi and someone jumps ahead of you in the queue, how would you react? Most people react by feeling annoyed. Some might get angry and shout at the person to get back in line.

The popular belief is that it is normal to feel annoyed, upset

You are Not your Thoughts

and angry when someone behaves badly. Is there any logic behind this belief? Where did you learn that it is normal for you to punish yourself with negative feelings such as anger, irritation, resentment, annoyance or frustration when somebody misbehaves?

In this chapter, I invite you to test the meaning and usefulness of the thinking patterns that limit your choices in small, everyday situations. How would it be for you if you were aware of how you motivated yourself? You may find that problems you blamed on your partner became issues because of the choices you unconsciously made.

When you want to feel better, improve your relationship, or change your behaviour, looking at how you think is the best place to start. Your thoughts help to define your mood in any given situation. Whenever you name and experience a mood, there is a thought connected to it that helps define the mood. Suppose you are having a conversation with your partner. When you are talking, your partner doesn't look at you but glances over your shoulder. Whether you feel ignored, irritated, hurt, sad, nervous or any other emotion will depend on what you think.

If you think your partner is rude, insulting you by not making eye contact, you might feel hurt and irritated. You might assume that he or she is not paying attention because he or she is distracted and has something serious in mind, and your reaction is to feel nervous and caring. Different thoughts and interpretations of an event will lead to different moods and reactions in the same situation.

This is why it is so important to identify what you are thinking and to check out the accuracy of the thoughts that put you in a good or bad mood. Your thoughts help you name the emotions you experience in each situation. Feelings are accompanied by additional thoughts that support and strengthen your moods.

The stronger a negative emotion is, the more extreme a person's thinking is likely to be. The thought is never wrong but acting on the thought might be unwise. An angry person who feels vulnerable may get satisfaction from thinking about hurting someone or damaging their property but not act on the thought. To imagine you do something to relieve strong feelings, without acting on the thought, can give emotional release.

Angry people are hurt people who want something they are not getting. Some of the many reasons why people feel angry include feeling under attack, not being respected, being treated unfairly and feeling powerless to do anything about a relationship or situation.

When you have very strong feelings, you are more likely to distort, discount or ignore information that contradicts your emotions or beliefs. You have a physical reaction to your thoughts. A frightening thought can lead to a more rapid heartbeat. Imagining a romantic scene can lead to sexual arousal.

Most clients are aware of whether physical sensations in the body feel good or bad. Tight shoulders or tension in the body may signal that a person is anxious, tired or afraid. A heavy feeling may indicate that someone feels depressed, disappointed or anticipates something unpleasant that they expect to happen.

Moods are often described by one word such as good or bad. Clients who find it difficult to name their emotions can be coached to extend their vocabulary from good and bad to happy and unhappy, annoyed or pleased. By developing an awareness of your emotional state, you will learn about connecting your thoughts and feelings.

9

DEFENCE MECHANISMS

When you show up as your authentic self, whatever that may be, you allow others to do the same, creating the world we all deserve.

SHANNA KATZ KATTARI

Wouldn't it be amazing to have an in-depth understanding of why we don't do what we tell ourselves we should do and genuinely want to do? In all of our lives there comes a point when we make the choice to get real and allow others to see who we really are. Kristin Neff, PhD, is a pioneer in self-compassion research. She says, 'Self-compassion is simply the process of turning compassion inward. We are kind and understanding rather than harshly self-critical when we fail, make mistakes or feel inadequate. We give ourselves support and encouragement rather than being cold and judgemental when challenges and difficulty arise in our lives.'

People believe their own internal dialogue. They make assumptions about their partner's motives. Learning to check out the accuracy of their own internal dialogue and practising reframing allows clients to develop a healthier sense of self-esteem, self-worth and in the process their self-confidence grows.

A challenge that every client who is willing to 'get real' faces is the threat to the ego. People want to feel they are right. It feels like a punch in the gut to discover how often you were wrong when you believed you were in the right. Ideally, for every one negative interaction, there should be five positive interactions, and this is easier said than done.

Many of us say one thing and then do another. We pay

lip-service to honouring our values and living with integrity, but some of our actions demonstrate that we have double standards. In my book, this is called 'being human'.

What do you do when life gives you lemons? You make lemonade. A positive can-do attitude is a gift in the face of apparent adversity. The creative person who set out to make the best of a bad situation will frequently end up with something that is positive, desirable and unexpected.

What does the oyster do when it's irritated by a grain of sand? It makes a beautiful pearl. In response to the discomfort, the oyster makes a smooth, protective coating, which encases the sand. Some pearls can develop in a period of six months. Others take up to four years to develop, which is why they have more value in the jewellery market.

No one gets through life without suffering emotional pain. With the benefits of hindsight, many of us learn that even though we would never want to revisit the events that caused us to suffer, we coped and found the inner strengths to survive and move on with life. Questions I ask clients so that they can learn important life lessons from adversity are:

- How did you grow stronger through coping with that difficulty?
- What resources did you find in yourself that allowed you to survive that crisis?
* What was it in you that helped you to survive so elegantly and beautifully?

I'm making an educated guess that you may not find this an easy chapter to read because I will be writing about ways we avoid dealing with painful emotions. Living with integrity and honouring our values sounds wonderful, but it is a huge challenge. If you are like me, you will find yourself reverting to old habits that you know do not serve you well. There will be many times when you will be tempted and opt to take the easy way out, to compromise your beliefs, or simply give up.

I don't deny that it's difficult to stand up for what you believe in, especially if it makes you see yourself as the odd one out. A surprising number of the commonly used self-protective and defence mechanisms we use are obstacles to happiness. They may appear to work well in the short term, but in the longer term they do not serve us well.

Projection is a highly effective defence mechanism. It involves unconsciously taking unwanted emotions or traits you don't like about yourself and attributing them to a partner. The old saying, 'We see others not as they are but as we are' gives a perfect explanation of projection, which is the mental process by which we attribute to others what is in our own minds.

As I learn to observe what is going on inside of me, I begin to understand myself better. This gives me insights into the issues I have with myself and with my partner and allows me to figure out how to make better decisions. When clients go through the process of looking at their own narrative, many discover that their emotional responses make perfect sense.

Finding out that there are good reasons for why they feel dissatisfied, not as happy and content as they want to be, offers reassurance to clients. For many, it confirms the emerging beliefs: 'There is nothing wrong with me. I did the best I could in the circumstances.' When outdated thinking is reframed, clients increase their sense of self-esteem.

A client's self-protective mechanisms do not change quickly because what they are attempting to do is change many of the unconscious patterns of a lifetime. Breaking old habits that served us well in the past is not easy, but the benefits make it worth the effort. Understanding why the self-protective and defence mechanisms used in the past do not serve us well on the quest for happiness is a sign of progress.

We use self-defence mechanisms as a protective measure from a perceived threat. If I feel frustrated and remain silent, my energy is divided between expressing myself and inhibiting myself from speaking. If I hold back because I'm afraid of upsetting my partner, it's likely that I fear some unpleasant consequence.

Have you any awareness of the part fear plays in limiting your choices? When you stop yourself from doing something you were thinking of doing or saying clearly what you needed to express, it's generally fear that's stopping you. What would you discover if you were to use your imagination and give it free rein? Think of the worst thing that could happen if you spoke out. What is the best thing that could happen if you allowed yourself to stop censoring and expressed yourself freely?

When you pay attention to what you are thinking, you wake up to the power in you to think differently and to look at things from many different perspectives. You may believe you have good reasons for not saying what you mean. Perhaps something is bothering you. You don't want to make a big issue out of it so you rationalise that the best policy is to keep quiet.

The best option when you are not sure about what to do is to do nothing. You can only resolve a problem when you are clear in yourself about how you feel and what you want to do. What makes this complex is that a part of you identifies with your feelings and wants. Another part identifies with your projections, catastrophising about what your partner might do, or fearing that you may live to regret something you might do, or say.

Defence Mechanisms

It's a good idea to clear up the inner struggle by working with the different parts of you that are in conflict before you decide on the way forward. If you believe that your issues are with your partner, you can do very little except complain or set out to make changes. When you recognise that much of the struggle and conflict are in you, you can stop blaming your partner for problems that are of your own making.

A first step is to become aware of the strategies you use to get what you want that are ineffective. When you learn why many of the strategies you use are unproductive, you can do something about them. For example, if you think that you can't talk about what is really bothering you, your partner is left in a no-win situation.

You may believe that you are communicating with your partner in a positive way because you say what you think in a nice way. Communication is a two-way process. Talking without paying attention to the effect what you say has on your partner is a one-way process, which may be motivated by anxiety.

Anxiety is an emotion the body feels when it is preparing for a challenge that is not there in reality. Many of us spend much of our lives catastrophising about things that will never happen and wishing for things that will never occur. Not saying what you mean, making something else the issue, and nagging are common strategies that never achieve the intended outcome.

A partner's defence mechanism may be to switch off and become deaf when there is constant chatter. If one partner has the attitude that they always know best, that it's their way or no way, communication becomes a one-way process.

Not saying what you mean is a recipe for confusion, misunderstanding and frustration. Trust is damaged whether your partner believes what you said or senses you are hiding something.

It may not be what you say, but the way you say it that gets your partner's back up. A whiney, angry or cold tone of voice can make your partner not want to hear the message.

There is a natural drive in all of us to want more, but we go about getting it in the wrong way. Nagging, going on and on about something you want, is never productive. Contrary to popular belief, nagging is a common habit in both men and women. You may think you are asking for what you want in a positive and respectful way. However, if you are repeating the same thing over and over again, it will sound like you're nagging. This is not communicating effectively.

There are ways to communicate without nagging, blaming or criticising. Blaming is a disguised form of criticism. If what your partner does or does not do upsets you, you have a perfect right to say so. 'I felt frustrated when I saw the mugs left on the counter' gives a very different message to 'You make me so frustrated when you leave the mugs on the counter'.

Putting your partner on the defensive by complaining, blaming or criticising creates an additional problem and is no way to find the solution you hope to achieve. Criticising your partner because you have a negative feeling is unlikely to get you the outcome you desire. Appreciating your partner for trying to keep the kitchen tidy is much more likely to have a positive outcome.

Changing the subject is a popular defence mechanism that is used if a partner talks too much or sounds like they are nagging. This can be most frustrating for the partner who wants to talk about something that is important to them. It can be demoralising to go into the narrative that maybe your partner doesn't care, is not interested, or is bored with you or the topic. Another possibility is that your partner finds it safer to change the subject rather than retreat into silence.

Making something else the issue is a safe way to avoid talking about what is bothering your partner. Deflecting by focusing on something else or complaining about some trivial issue is another defence mechanism. It's a way of distracting from the real issue. The trouble with changing the subject and deflecting is it's unproductive. The trivial issue may be dealt with satisfactorily, but the real problem remains untouched.

It's natural for people to want something better, whether they know what that 'something' is or not. The desire to feel fit and healthy is universal. Everyone knows what to do – choose a healthy diet, take exercise and avoid junk food. Despite knowing the right thing to do, many of us continue to eat junk food, live a sedentary lifestyle and avoid exercise like the plague.

Some people who go through a major health crisis are motivated to change their diets and set out to live a healthier lifestyle. Others start out well but soon drift back to their old habits. Those who succeed in eliminating junk food from their diets, eat healthy foods and take regular exercise do well. They won't find this fun – change never is, but the rewards are more than worth the effort.

Clients who want a healthier mindset need to work hard to discard 'junk thinking' and practise reframing. People who work on compassionate self-understanding quickly learn to recognise their negative narratives. Those who are kind, tolerant and compassionate with themselves do very well.

The transformation when clients develop an understanding of why they are dissatisfied, discontented and unfulfilled is a joy to see. Seeing the world from a different perspective makes so many changes that once seemed unthinkable possible. Understanding brings clarity of perception, which leads to accuracy of response.

There is no denying that poor relationship modelling leads to a fundamental misunderstanding about how people in happy couples relate to their partners. Psychologist John O. Stevens says, 'All of us carry around part of our "past" with us in memories. Our memories, even if they are exact images of previous events and things, are images and not the events themselves.'

I'm making an educated guess that when your inner parts are struggling because they want different things, at least one part will sound like a parent. Before you can let go of a memory, you will have to find out what it does for you and what you gain by hanging on to it. If the memory is unpleasant, there is probably an unfinished situation where you held yourself back from expressing yourself fully.

How strongly you feel emotions has a lot to do with your personality type. If you grew up feeling it was wrong to feel negative emotions, you may have pushed them down so deep that you are no longer aware of them. Or you might have unconsciously changed them to something else. A woman who fears anger may turn it inwards and feel depressed. A man who is afraid of looking weak may sound loud and aggressive to hide this.

Guilt is a natural response when we misbehave and are caught doing something that we are not supposed to do. Shame tends to be connected to my own narrative, thinking if others found out what I have done, they would think badly of me. When we feel shame, we view ourselves in a negative way.

Sometimes shame is instilled in childhood by authority figures. The belief that there is something wrong with me, in some way I am flawed, makes it difficult to develop a healthy sense of self-esteem. Who has never been told, 'You should be ashamed of yourself'? Statements such as, 'You shouldn't feel that way', 'You'll never be as good as your cousin', 'You're a selfish brat' may not be uttered with the intention of scarring a child's sense of who he or she is. What shaming does is give a powerful message that is soul-destroying.

Many of my clients are trustworthy, reliable and honest people. The decisions they made throughout their lives were made with the very best of intentions. I'm confident that in every situation where they have regrets, they did their very best. When figuring out what they did and why they acted in ways they now feel remorseful about, I caution them to do so without judgement or approval.

The truth is we live with a certain idea of who we are and how we should behave that is part of our programming. It's said that we become what others tell us we are. We're influenced by the people closest to us in ways we understand and in ways we will never understand. What no one told us was that burying unwanted feelings and avoiding unpleasantness takes a certain amount of energy, which limits our freedom to be fully ourselves.

Fear of missing out (FOMO) is a modern phenomenon. It isn't a diagnosable psychological condition yet, but it has been shown to directly impact both mental and physical health. Do you think that the feeling that you are missing something fundamentally important that others are experiencing right now is an obstacle to happiness and fulfilment?

Is it possible that living with the sense of missing the kind of happiness that you see others experiencing may generate feelings of discontent, diminish your sense of wellbeing and fulfilment with your partner and with life in general? If your answer is 'yes', I have another question. Are you telling me that you want to feel what you believe the happy couples you want to feel like, feel?

Are you really missing the happiness your heart desires? Could it be that you are happier than you realise? Might it be the thought that something is missing which generates feelings of discontent in you? Is it possible that if your focus is on what you are missing, you are giving yourself a general sense of disappointment and failing to appreciate what you have but do not value?

No one can go through life without experiencing uncomfortable, unpleasant and emotionally upsetting experiences. In the measure that you try to avoid negative experiences, your awareness is reduced. When you understand that it's not your partner but your responses to your own internal dialogue that make you feel disappointed, frustrated or anxious, you are ready to become the master of your fate.

Some clients derive great benefits from self-observation. Others are not yet ready to get fully involved in cultivating self-awareness. When uncomfortable truths emerge, they prefer to hang on to the image they have of themselves rather than take the risk of being challenged to think in new ways and take responsibility for their own happiness.

'Integrity' is not a word that you hear very often today and it's easier to spell out what it is not, rather than attempt to define what it is. At a basic level, people who fail to keep their promises or meet their commitments, lie, let others take the blame for their mistakes or point the finger of blame at anyone to avoid taking responsibility are lacking in integrity.

At the top level, you find the unscrupulous, corrupt people who engage in criminal fraud. They lack any moral code. Everything they do is for personal gain. They leave a trail of destruction behind them, destroying lives and livelihoods. Today, integrity has become such a rare commodity that politicians who are known to be corrupt have been elected as presidents of their countries.

I tell my clients that no good purpose is served by burdening yourself with regrets for the past. It's a waste of energy to hold on to feelings of guilt and shame. Admit that there were many times when you failed to live up to the standards of behaviour you aspired to but did not reach.

Overcoming guilt and shame does not mean letting yourself off the hook. Taking an appropriate amount of responsibility and coming to terms with whatever motivation led you to feel those emotions is the key to moving forward on the happiness quest.

Guilt for what happened in the past is the one emotion I have no time for, and the work I do with clients to let go of their guilt is very freeing. Dealing with feelings of guilt is like removing layers to get to the core issue. On the top layer are expectations. Have you any concept of the myriad of expectations that you are attempting to live up to?

You have expectations of yourself. Your partner has expectations of you. Think of all the other people in your life you interact with – children if you have them, siblings, parents, cousins, friends, colleagues, shopkeepers, doctors, police, the butcher, the baker, the candlestick maker. They all have expectations of you.

Add to this all the written and unwritten rules you feel you must keep. Obey the police, don't drink and drive, keep the rules of the road, pay your taxes, etc. It may sound crazy to think that there are intelligent adults who feel guilty for making a teacher whom they haven't seen in decades angry and upset with them. When you were a child, your teacher told you when to sit and where to hang your coat and you were taught to comply.

It would be remiss of me not to mention that some people are skilled in creating guilt in others to manipulate them. Tears can be a genuine outpouring of grief. They can also be used as a defence mechanism to avoid culpability. For example, the woman who bursts into tears and the man who presents as a victim can manipulate others into feeling guilty about confronting them when they appear upset.

When any part of you experienced a demand to live up to expectations that you were unable to meet, you learned to feel bad. The message you gave yourself was something like, 'I can't measure up to expectations. I'm inadequate. I'm not good enough. There is something wrong with me.'

'Make me proud' is an unreasonable parental demand, which may be impossible to achieve. The demand to live up to expectations puts a child under pressure. Even if one accepts that the demands made were reasonable and admits they could easily be satisfied, the pressure to meet parents' expectations is likely to generate resentment.

I don't know what word you would use for the bad feeling you give yourself when you fail to live up to your own expectations. I'm going to cluster all those negative feelings about demands that clients failed to meet under the word 'resentment'. So, let's recap. At the surface layer, there are expectations that are experienced as demands. The narrative around finding it impossible to live up to expectations generates negative thoughts. Believing you are unable to meet the demands made on you will frequently generate feelings of resentment.

Layers of resentment that are not dealt with turn into what I call toxic guilt. In small quantities, you do not feel the effects of a toxic substance. Once the toxicity reaches a tipping point, you feel the unpleasant effects. In my experience, symptoms of toxic guilt include shame, poor self-image, self-blaming, insomnia, anxiety, stress, migraines, nausea, stomach problems and fatigue.

Fantasy exercises are a wonderful teaching tool for helping clients learn what happens in them when they have buried resentment and guilt. Learning what compliance does for them as well as to them offers valuable insights. 'For what purpose did you comply even though you would prefer not to?' is a powerful question for uncovering the self-protective motivation of a client.

Engaging fully in a fantasy exercise offers clients an easy and unthreatening way to let go of guilt, shame and resentment. When a fantasy is allowed to develop on its own without manipulation, it will take on a life of its own. I recall doing an exercise on releasing resentment with a woman who told me that she used curse words in the exercise that she didn't even know she knew.

This is the exercise to release guilt and shame. Find a quiet place and time when you won't be disturbed. Recall just one incident when you experienced guilty feelings. It can be a recent event or something from any time in your life. Just make sure that you select just one event and stay with it all through the exercise.

Imagine yourself back in the situation as if it were happening right now. Use all of your senses to do this. Look around you and see what you see. Hear what you hear. Pay attention to everything, what you see and hear and smell. Recall all the details of the situation. Where are you? Is there anyone there with you? What happens? What exactly do you feel guilty about? What is happening physically in your body?

Now think of the one person that you would least like to tell about your guilt. Pick someone who would be most upset, judgemental or angry if he or she knew about it. Imagine this person is here facing you. Visualise the person. Take in all the details. What is the person wearing? What kind of facial expression does the person have? Are they standing or sitting?

Imagine that you talk to the person and tell them exactly what you feel guilty about. Express yourself honestly and directly. Start by saying, 'I'm going to tell you about something I did.' Notice how you feel as you do this. When you have done this, you change places.

Become the other person and talk to yourself as if you were the other person. What do you say in response to hearing these things? How do you feel as you respond to the 'guilty you'? It's common to find resentment behind the guilt. If you acted in opposition to your partner's wishes, the resentment might be, 'I resent you telling me what to do. I resent you not listening to what I want.'

Express the resentments in the incident you feel guilty about. Don't mince your words. Get whatever you need to say off your chest. How do you feel as you do this? Is there anything else you want to say? Again, change places and respond to what was said as if you are the other person.

Become the person responding to the resentments you expressed. Do your very best to get the feel of being the other person. What do you say? As you respond to the resentment, how do you feel physically in your body? The dialogue in these kinds of exercises can go on for a long time, with the client changing places more than once.

Everything you experience in this exercise happens in your own mind. Whatever occurs between the 'guilty you' and the 'other person' occurs in different parts of you. If there is conflict in your dialogue, and you start off feeling alienated from 'the

DEFENCE MECHANISMS

other', the conflict is in you, between different parts of you.

The monumental life lesson to be learned from this type of interior work is that in the past, we wrongly assumed that our problems, issues and conflicts were with our partner and other people. The struggle that we went through, when we felt pressurised by the expectations and demands of others, generated feelings of suffering, pain and distress.

Initially, it's hard for clients to fully accept that much of what they believe is a fantasy, a story that exists in their minds. The emotional distress within the client is real, but it does not exist in present ongoing reality. Change the story and you change the emotional response.

This is not an easy concept to accept when you are reading words in a book. The turning point for the clients who were sceptical before the exercise comes afterwards, when they experience the freedom that comes from letting go.

Have you clarity about what is working well and what is not emotionally healthy for you in your partnership? It is not emotionally healthy to put on a smile and act as if everything is okay when it is not. Putting your partner's needs and wishes ahead of your own is often the coping strategy of someone who lacks self-esteem and who has a low sense of self-worth.

When you understand why you act as you do, you will develop the flexibility to act appropriately in different situations and feel confident that you have the capacity to respond accurately. It may not always be wise to express how you feel when you experience any kind of negative or resentful feeling, even if you were to do so in a respectful way. Before you say anything, go inside and look for clarity about why you think a demand is being made of you. Clarity usually brings an accuracy of perception, and quite often an effortless response.

A turning point in many people's lives happens when they get clarity about what is not emotionally healthy in their interaction with themselves and others. Understanding that it is not emotionally healthy to put on a smile and act as if everything is okay when it is not makes for more honest relationships. The gift in understanding and reframing misguided beliefs about introspection, self-appreciation and selfishness is the growth in courage and self-confidence that follows.

10

HOLDING YOURSELF ACCOUNTABLE WITH A LIGHT TOUCH

The greater danger for most of us lies not in setting our aim too high and falling short. But in setting our aim too low, and achieving our mark.

MICHELANGELO

Effective life coaching allows clients to discover who they are and where they are in their lives as well as in their careers. The goal of organisations that send clients for career coaching may be to make them better managers, to improve their ability to negotiate or develop interpersonal relationship skills.

Regardless of the agenda that is brought to coaching, the bottom line is that every client wants change in one or more areas of their lives. Clients don't live their lives in discrete compartments. Valued employees may excel in their work lives while other areas of their lives are chaotic.

As people live integrated lives, putting effort into personal growth is bound to have a positive effect in every area of a person's personal, professional, and social life. An ethical decision that some coaches make is to inform the organisation that there is an outside possibility that as a result of the coaching process, one of their people may decide they want a change of career.

Some clients act as if their work life and home life are disconnected. In some ways, it can be helpful to compartmentalise. But isn't it true that people bring their work frustrations home with them and their relationship issues to work? Family problems influence a person's performance at work. Concerns about a sick child or wanting to get to the hospital in time to be with a partner who is about to give birth will take the focus off work.

Many outwardly very successful people have done what society programmed them to do. They worked hard and focused on advancing their career sometimes to the detriment of their partnership and family life. There is no denying that all work and no play makes for a pretty poor quality of life. A positive outcome from the Covid-19 lockdown was the tsunami of people who reassessed their priorities and found merit in working less to spend more time with the family, even if this meant a lower standard of living.

Dr Arthur Brooks is a Harvard professor who teaches courses on happiness. He believes that the secret to being more satisfied is not having more, it's having less. I saw this very clearly with one man I coached who had his own business. He had all the outward symbols of a successful career. He owned the sports car with the personalised number plate, had three holidays a year and a mansion of a house. Yet he was one of the unhappiest clients I have ever coached. I enquired how he really felt about himself when he was alone. I will never forget his answer. He said, 'I feel like s—t'.

At one time, I used to invite clients to name their values. In hindsight, that was a futile exercise. Human nature being what it is, clients tended to name off a list of the values they believed people should have and exclude values that might show them up in a bad light. My best wisdom as I gained coaching experience was to go back to the 'show don't tell' method.

Because our language is so imprecise I will attempt to clarify what I mean by my use of the word 'values'. Values are intangible. Most of us can walk into a room full of strangers and within a few minutes assume we know a lot about the people there. Their clothing, hairstyle, posture and attitude may give us a hint about their values and personality. But the outward appearance of a person cannot define nor determine what values the person holds.

Clients can find it surprisingly difficult to observe themselves without judgement or approval. Setting out to have peace of mind and feel fulfilled, happy and content is a part of the journey that can't be rushed. You build the life changes you want step by step. Some who take an honest look at how they interact with a partner, family and friends have to admit to themselves that some of their behaviour is not in line with their values.

Some clients discover they are way out of their comfort zones when they figure out that they are personally responsible for so much of what they say they don't want in their lives. People believe they know themselves because they are familiar with their own predictable patterns of behaviour. Yet if asked 'What's going on inside of you?' they have difficulty answering. There are good reasons for this.

I feel huge respect for the bravery of clients who have the self-discipline to keep their commitments. Can an unfit person, who does not take exercise regularly, succeed in the goal to climb Mount Kilimanjaro? Of course not, and the client who sets out to achieve personal goals will not succeed unless they are willing to put in the time and necessary effort to achieve success.

There is truth in the saying, 'no gain without pain'. Hard work is necessary to achieve any goal. Dropping old habits and building new ones is challenging because change takes people out of their comfort zones. Frequently, there is a level of discomfort and maybe pain for the unfit person who sets out to build up stamina, gain strength and improve cardiovascular fitness.

To have the self-discipline to set and maintain any exercise regime is never easy. The motivation to succeed is huge for the climber who has sponsors that had to be convinced that reaching the summit was an achievable goal. To reach the level of fitness required to climb a mountain, the climber must maintain a daily exercise regime.

Integrity and moral values are closely related concepts. Integrity involves consistency in one's actions, and thoughts, even when faced with challenges, temptations and the desire to quit. Values provide a moral and ethical framework.

'If you want to change the world, start off by making your bed' is the most famous line from a speech given by William H. McRaven, a retired US Navy admiral. To make your bed to perfection each morning is a reminder to live by the dictates of your own integrity.

You honour your values and show integrity when you do the little things that no one is going to see. In the overall scheme of things, doing your daily meditation practice may appear to be insignificant, but trust me – it makes big changes possible.

To have the integrity to hold yourself accountable shows you are self-aware. Self-awareness is one's ability to perceive and understand how one's thoughts, emotions and actions are generated. The self-aware person intuits the reason why they desire to numb themselves to certain emotions when they feel vulnerable. They may have issues with a fear of judgement, rejection and not being liked. By coping with their fears, they will improve their self-esteem and build up self-confidence.

Holding Yourself Accountable with a Light Touch

One way to develop self-awareness is to practise mindfulness and meditation. Daily practice takes commitment and dedication. Here is a very simple awareness exercise that I used with clients for decades before mindfulness became popular. It offers what I believe is 'breathing space'. How you use this space is up to you. You may choose to use it as a mindfulness practice, a breath meditation or a prayer meditation:

- Take a moment to be fully present to yourself.
- Make sure you are sitting comfortably.
- Now pay attention to your breathing.
- Don't change how you breathe.
- If your breathing is shallow, leave it that way.
- Make no attempt to deepen the breath.
- Just be aware of the air as it enters and leaves the nostrils.
- Notice if you are breathing through one nostril or two.
- Whatever you aware of is perfect for you.

If you wish to pray, put yourself in the presence of God before you begin. In breath meditation and prayer, the thoughts that come into the mind unbidden are regarded as distractions. The moment you notice a distraction, smile and return to the breath. The tendency to be judgemental dissolves when you include the practice of 'smilingly return to the breath'.

In a mindfulness practice, you begin with the relaxation part of the exercise. As you relax, your breathing thoughts will appear. If you are not looking to engage with the thoughts, you can simply watch them as you would watch the clouds floating across the sky. Some thoughts you may like and want to focus on. Others you may find disturbing.

You can choose to focus on a thought or let it drift away like a cloud floating across the sky. It's your decision. Stay with a thought or a feeling if you wish to have a better understanding of your thought patterns, emotions and reactions. As little as five minutes a day spent on mindfulness practice is of benefit in cultivating self-awareness.

If you are new to any of these practices, I suggest that you spend a minimum of a month practising for maybe five or a maximum of ten minutes before you increase the time. Always use a timer. The logic behind limiting the time is that when you are enjoying the experience, the natural inclination is to increase the time. A danger if you extend the time and it doesn't feel good is you will shorten the time and soon drop the practice.

When clients have issues with their partners I often ask, 'How frequently do you avoid communicating about the real issues?' Time and time again, I hear the story of the irritable and frustrated partner who makes an inaccurate attribution, projects it onto the other partner and has a perception that it is coming from them.

I see partners making the same mistakes over and over again. Some couples place themselves in situations where they are bound to have a row. They seem to be blind to how they set up the situations that always end with conflict. I know that couples who fight must be meeting some need, otherwise the rows wouldn't reoccur. My best wisdom when this is reported is to ask, 'How do the decisions you made when that happened impact on what you want in the future?'

The challenge when you pay close attention to how you interact with yourself and others is the insights you gain into the defence mechanisms you use. Knowledge is the key to managing your life better. In that process, you will become familiar with many challenges. You will come face to face with what you fear or avoid. 'FEAR' could stand for 'feel everything and recover'.

Holding Yourself Accountable with a Light Touch

Is there a fear response in you when you are invited to take stock of where you are in your life today? Let me ask you: What is your relationship with yourself like right now? What is your first thought when answering this question? The first thought is usually the uncensored one.

I know this sounds complicated but please bear with me. I encourage clients to develop their curiosity and creativity. I invite them to observe what they learn from paying attention to the narrative that comes after their first thought. The benefits they gain from being curious are that it motivates their desire to learn, explore new things, seek knowledge, ask questions, and challenge conventional norms.

I could tell you that intelligent people possess problem-solving skills. That may be true, but problems are unlikely to be resolved if the people with the problems do not attribute the same meaning to the words or jargon they use.

I want clients to overcome any antipathy they have to learning how to be more curious. Curiosity can be a helpful resource. It helps clients understand how their unconscious use of defence mechanisms may have hurt their partner in the past. It allows them to see how their actions have the potential to cause hurt and upset. Nosy, inquisitive people who look for gossip, and pry into other people's business have an unhealthy curiosity.

Feeling curious about where your thoughts come from will allow you to become aware of distorted perceptions. Misunderstanding, misinterpretations and assumptions can generate a great deal of emotional suffering. In the process of 'peeling the onion skins' and reflecting on what happened and why, clients are alerted to habitual doubts and fears.

It's empowering to learn about the unconscious defence mechanisms we use automatically, which stop us being our best selves. For example, keeping silent, not admitting that something is bothering you when it is, nagging, changing the subject, being sarcastic, criticising, and not listening are some of the most-used defence mechanisms.

These are only the beginning of a very long list. Silence in some circumstances can be the wisest course of action. In others, it may be an unwise decision that perpetuates what a person does not want. And in some cases, may be a missed opportunity for an honest conversation.

If I remain silent or deny that something is wrong when my partner clearly sees there is an issue, it shows a lack of trust in the partnership. Not talking about the real issue is an avoidance measure. Some clients, who are not brave enough to spell out what's bothering them, make something else the issue to relieve their feelings. Usually, they pick some trivial inconvenience to focus on, such as constantly losing the car keys.

Trivial issues around lost keys can be easily rectified by either putting up a hook to hang them on or getting a second set of keys. However, if unresolved, the real issues will continue to generate unhappiness and a lack of contentment. Contentious issues have a habit of multiplying. It is common for a client who is curious about why they feel a certain way to become aware of how the defence mechanism of avoidance has a major role in keeping issues alive.

Changing the subject and deflecting is another method of avoidance. If the topic of conversation gets uncomfortable or the person is not really interested in having a discussion, they change the direction of the interaction. This can be infuriating for a partner. A more positive and honest way to act is to say it like it is:

- I don't want to talk about this yet.
- It's too hard for me to have this conversation right now.

- If it's okay with you, can we talk about something else?

One definition of sarcasm is the use of irony to mock or convey contempt. Let's not deny or ignore the fact that sarcasm can be hurtful, offensive and diminish a partner. I don't deny that sarcastic comments can sound clever and funny and make others laugh. However, humour can be used as a weapon to inflict pain. Sarcasm as a defence mechanism is an effective way to hide insecurity or look for power.

Criticism can have a devastating effect on a partnership and it will never get a person the results they want. Repeated criticism can shake a person's confidence, put them on the defensive and generate more problems. Some couples' fights grow into an escalating pattern where criticism reappears with greater frequency and intensity. Making comments and judgments about a partner's flaws, blaming and complaining are disguised forms of criticism.

Repeated criticism chips away at a person's self-esteem and sense of self-worth. It will cause a person to question their own values if it comes from a partner who is supposed to love and cherish them. The confidence of the recipient is eroded until eventually they may begin to doubt their own abilities.

A right-fighter who needs their opinion to prevail may interrupt and contradict a partner. Not allowing someone to finish what they are saying is bad manners and disrespectful. Partners who are not resolving their differences often have bitter rows that follow a pattern of interrupting and shouting over each other. When fighting descends into a shouting match, both parties lose out.

Living with a partner who insists on being right, even when they are wrong, is incredibly stressful. It's normal for things to get heated in an argument. However, a controlling person who sets out to bully, demean, humiliate and deceive a partner just to win an argument could be showing narcissistic tendencies.

A narcissist never takes responsibility for their actions. If anything bad happens, it is blamed on someone else. Their wants, needs and expenses are the priority. They lure their partner in by being charming and attentive. Very quickly, they show their tendencies. They twist things, lie, dismiss what is said, treat others positively and demean their partner. At an extreme level, they may become aggressive. Name-calling, personal insults, lying and mocking behaviour from a partner who laughs at you when you express hurt or collapse into tears is abusive.

Our defence mechanisms are built up over a lifetime. They start for one reason and will frequently continue long after their original purpose is served. We use defence mechanisms to make us feel better and avoid painful feelings.

Denial is one of the most common defence mechanisms. When a situation or fact becomes too much to handle, the coping mechanism is to refuse to experience it. By denying reality, you are essentially protecting yourself from having to face and deal with confusion, unpleasant consequences, or emotional pain. Suppressing our feelings will block the natural flow of emotions.

When you trace something back to its source, you may find that you learned to remain silent for one reason. Maybe a parent told you that you talked too much and from that you learned that silence protected you. Remaining quiet started for one reason and continued for a myriad of other reasons.

Most of us are under the impression that we are coping well. In some areas of our lives, we are but there is no doubt that there are times when we react automatically without thinking. It's easier to focus on the areas of my life that are working well than to look at what is not working.

Holding Yourself Accountable with a Light Touch

When partners have issues and don't talk about their feelings, two things happen. The first is they make assumptions about what their partner thinks and feels. The second is they look at how their partner behaves and often misinterpret the other's motivation or intentions.

Our blind spots are the things we do or say that other people see about us, but we remain unaware of them. You may have heard the old saying that one man's meat is another man's poison. Nagging falls into this category. One partner has a perception that they have a positive attitude when they ask for something. Their assumption is that they ask nicely but occasionally have to remind their partner. Their partner gets tired of hearing them go on and on, repeating the same request over and over again.

Nagging is repeatedly telling your partner what you think should be done. It never gets a person what they want. Constant nagging poisons couple relationships. It has the effect of making a partner want to shut out what they are tired of hearing.

Saying something about how you feel and why you feel that way is an important part of communication. Telling your partner what to do or how to behave is not. If your partner hurts your feelings, you have a right to explain why you feel upset. But if you keep repeating the same words over and over again, you are not communicating effectively.

When you observe yourself and pay attention to your own personal narrative, it is highly probable that the thoughts 'I'm not loved', 'I'm not heard', or some derivative of these will emerge into consciousness. In most of our lives, thoughts such as these have been repeated thousands and thousands of times. Why not challenge your internal dialogue? If you change the narrative, you will immediately change how you feel.

Relationship researcher John Gottman promotes the idea

of the five-to-one ratio. For every one negative feeling or interaction between partners, there must be five positive feelings or interactions. You will quickly discover the power of reframing when you begin to appreciate and value your own effort. Coaching clients to engage in compassionate self-care has enormous benefits.

By reframing, you challenge the negative thoughts and beliefs that contribute to your emotional distress. You become aware of distortions in your thoughts. Changing the negative dialogue that does not serve you well will alter how you think and feel. It will empower you to generate a more positive and realistic way of thinking.

Feeling empowered builds resilience and self-confidence. It enables you to feel optimistic, have courage and be more focused on your goals. Changing the habitual actions of a lifetime involves the willingness to have a commitment to hard work. I tell clients, your partner's actions are one half of the story, but if you want to be happy, please keep the focus on yourself.

There is no magic formula for how to get your partner to listen and understand how you feel. Could the tone and volume of your voice be a reason you are not heard when you express yourself? Make the effort to speak in a calm, respectful manner. Nothing can get resolved if one partner shouts, gets angry, attacks or blames their partner.

Bursting into tears and becoming over-emotional may release negative feelings and get things off one's chest. It may shut down and end conversations, too. An ongoing irritant in many partnerships is that one partner believed they had a conversation to clear the air. They explained how they felt and what they needed as fully and honestly as they could. It never seemed to make a difference. There was no change in their partner's behaviour.

People will change only when they want to change and when they see that there is some reward for the new behaviour. The expectation that if a partner understands what you need, they will make the changes you desire, is not realistic.

Maybe you calmly explained how you felt more than once. You were confident that you gave your partner the time, space and safety to listen. You explained what you wanted and needed as clearly as you could. As you went through all of the above, did you wonder if it is fair to want someone to change how they behave because you want to feel a certain way?

Let's break it down. What if the message you communicate is, I want you to act in a certain way so that I feel good? Could that be construed as, I want you to change so that our partnership is happier? If a client answers 'yes' to either of these questions, it's clear that they have more work to do. They have yet to learn how to drop unrealistic expectations and to take full responsibility for their own happiness.

11

DEALING WITH INTERNAL CONFLICT

I'd rather regret the things I've done than regret the things I haven't done.

LUCILLE BALL

Our early childhood experiences have a profound impact on our intellectual, emotional and social development. They influence our adult beliefs, behaviours and values. Power struggles are a natural and normal part of a child's development. They occur when both a parent and child want to have their way and neither has any intention of backing down.

To compensate for feeling powerless, a child will often misbehave or refuse to comply with an adult. Unintentionally, parents reward this misbehaviour. They are more likely to notice and comment when a child misbehaves. When corrected, the child gets the attention they crave. For children, getting negative attention is better than no attention at all.

Seeking power is developmentally normal for children. If a parent constantly wins the power contest, the child may retaliate for the frustrations that arise when feeling controlled. A parent is caught up in a power struggle if a child is asked to do something and they consistently refuse to comply.

A lovely thing to do when a child is disobedient is to bend down, put your arm around them and ask, 'Why do you think I'm angry with you?' It's surprising how often the child has no idea. All they know is a parent is unhappy. If the disapproving parent followed up by saying, 'This is what I wish you would do instead.' It would help the child to understand what they did that was unacceptable.

A power struggle occurs when a wilful child is determined to have their way, and the adult insists it must be done their way. For example, a child who could dress unaided may revert to an earlier stage and look for help getting ready in the morning. Someone who used to put away their toys without being asked, has to be told repeatedly to tidy up. The non-verbal message is that the child will tidy up in their own time. In both instances, the children are using the power of non-compliance.

Parent/child conflict increases during adolescence. A young child doesn't have the capacity to work out the motivation behind the strategies they use when trying to take their power back. A teenager is more than capable of seeking revenge through passive-aggressive behaviour. Adolescents will show hostility indirectly rather than overtly. They hide their feelings of fear and vulnerability through non-compliance and hostile body language. They may procrastinate over tasks that they don't want to do and ignore chores which allow them to feel that they have a small measure of control.

Hardly any of us take the time to fully realise what is going on in us when we do what we really don't want to do. You're bound to experience inner turmoil if your parts are in conflict and you say 'yes' when you really want to say 'no'. Some clients spend much of their time complying, others are always compliant, and some give the appearance of complying when they're not.

As a child, you learned that if you didn't comply with what adults wanted, you would probably face unpleasant consequences. The fear of parental disapproval and the threat of punishment encouraged children to conceal feelings of frustration, hide the anger they were afraid to show, and bury the love they didn't know how to express.

There are many reasons why people repress emotions. Repression involves unconsciously blocking unwanted feelings. In childhood, repressing emotions was a protective mechanism. People commonly repress emotions they fear others might consider as negative, such as feelings of fear, resentment, frustration, grief and anger. Positive emotions such as excitement, joy and happiness are usually expressed openly.

It's good to be fully aware of what you are thinking and how you are feeling when you comply. If you have parts that want to comply and parts that don't, it's worth finding out why the parts are in conflict. Whether you really want to comply or not is your decision, or maybe it isn't. If you wish, you could write down the answers to the following questions:

- What are you aware of when you comply with a partner's wishes?
- What are you expressing?
- What are you holding back?
- What would you like to say if you had the freedom to express yourself?
- What blocks your self-expression?
- Pause and take the time you need to reflect on your answers.

Some people conform to expectations and they spend much of their time complying. Others give the appearance of complying when they're not. Which are you? A conformist is someone who behaves in a way that is considered acceptable by most people and who rarely does anything that would meet with disapproval. The two extremes of compliance are the conformist who always complies and the rebel who never complies.

Neuro-Linguistic Programming (NLP) teaches that there are two types of motivation that work in different ways. People either go towards what they want or away from what they don't want. They tend to be more biased towards one than the other. Everyone has developed 'toward' and 'away from' motivations. Both types of motivation have advantages and disadvantages.

At one extreme, a person may be so motivated to go towards a goal that they rush headlong into a project, working day and night, with little consideration for the effect on their partner. At the other extreme, the person with the 'away from' motivation may be too fearful to get started. They delay beginning a project until they are under some kind of pressure. Author Tony Robbins, one of the most famous coaches in the world, argues that there are only two things that motivate us to take action – inspiration and desperation.

If there are problems in your relationship with your partner, you can only deal with them when you are clear in yourself about how you feel and what you want to do. If you are in the habit of complying or conforming, you identify partly with your own feelings and wants and partly with the fantasy narratives you tell yourself that generate inner turmoil in you.

Imagine how you could feel if there was no need for you to comply, no pressure to conform. What if you believed that if others have expectations of you, their expectations belong to them? You are under no obligation to live up to their expectations. Wouldn't this thinking make you the master or mistress of your own life, free to express yourself in any way you choose?

Psychologists say our emotions are a source of information that alerts us to how we can remain safe, survive, and thrive. What you think of as negative emotions can feel unpleasant, uncomfortable and even painful at times. I tend to say 'so-called negative feelings' because some of our most uncomfortable emotions are designed with the intention of protecting us from harm.

Emotions are chemicals released in response to how we interpret specific triggers. This is why we say that emotions are neither good nor bad, they simply are. To be able to feel your feelings deeply is a gift because all emotions serve a purpose. It's helpful to think about emotions such as fear, frustration and anger as being on a spectrum that goes from low intensity to high intensity feelings. Apprehension and anxiety would be at the lower end of fear. Absolute terror would be at the top end, at the highest intensity.

Many of the decisions we make are fear-based. I regularly coach clients who have difficulty making decisions because they fear the consequences of making a choice. Fear is our most powerful emotion because it is a survival mechanism that dates to when we lived in caves.

It helps us become aware, identify and avoid threats to our safety. Fear is experienced in the mind and it triggers a physical reaction in the body. When you feel scared, anxious or apprehensive, you are responding to a perceived threat. Terror will trigger a powerful signal to warn of imminent danger.

Our brains are hardwired to act when fear is felt. The amygdala alerts the nervous system, which sets the fear response in the body in motion. The amygdala is an almond-shaped structure deep within the brain involved in processing emotion and memory. Writing about emotions will always bring up the inadequacy of language to describe a feeling.

Feelings are not facts that can be confirmed. They originate within you. Fear may stem from self-doubt, insecurities, concern about what your partner may think or from past experiences. In this book, you will find exercises that will empower you to make decisions that previously you may have feared making. The exercises are not difficult to do but many of them will challenge you to step out of your comfort zone. It takes determined personal work and immense courage and self-awareness to consistently ask and answer the question, 'What is behind the fear?'

I find many clients are perfectly comfortable with the idea that there are many different parts in them. They gain huge benefits from learning to pay close attention to their internal dialogue and talking to their different parts.

For example, a part loves the idea of regular exercise. Another part resists the thought of the exertion involved. A third part thinks it would be more relaxing to read or watch television. It's rare to find someone who is not aware of this kind of inner conflict.

Decades of research have shown that talking to oneself is completely normal. I have seen research that suggests that thirty to fifty per cent of people don't have internal monologues but I have yet to meet a person from this group.

We use internal dialogue to interpret the words we hear, process our thoughts, rehearse the conversations we imagine, and make decisions. It's common to hear people say, 'I tell myself' or 'I told myself'. It's natural for clients to confirm that they listen to themselves but I've yet to hear someone tell me that they are in the habit of listening to and hearing themselves.

The following is a simple exercise to guide you through how to work with your parts. It will take about three minutes for Part 1:

- Select a place where you feel comfortable and won't be disturbed.

- Begin by noticing what's going on in you.
- Notice the thoughts that come up for you.
- Are they pleasant or unpleasant?
- There is no right or wrong way to do this exercise. Whatever you are aware of is perfect for you.

I suggest you set a timer for ten minutes when you move on to Part 2. Spend a little time with each step:

- Notice how you respond to what you are thinking.
- Do you stay with one feeling more than the other?
- Just observe with no judgement.
- What thoughts or feelings do you like to focus on?
- What thoughts or feelings do you avoid?
- Focusing on one part is a way of not focusing or avoiding something else.
- Give a voice to your different parts.

When you give a voice to a part, it's like you talk to it as if it had a little personality of its own. Ask a question and listen for answers. The value of working with your parts is that every part in you is an aspect of yourself. When your parts want different things, you experience inner turmoil.

You may be happy to discover that every part, particularly the parts that you may have categorised as 'negative' are working for your good. At first, it may feel a little strange to talk to a thought or a feeling as if you were talking to another person. You will be pleasantly surprised at how quickly it feels natural.

Talking to my parts has become second-nature to me now. As I'm writing this, a part of me feels apprehensive about inviting readers to actively engage with the exercise. It will take me about a minute to demonstrate how I dialogue with the part. The first thing I do when working with a part is to take a moment to check in and ask if the part is willing to communicate with me. I like to thank the part when I get an answer.

I know that the part of me that feels apprehensive has a positive intention for me. Please can you tell me what the positive intention is, what good are you seeking for me?

To be aware of the fear of not being a clear communicator.

Thank you for communicating with me. What will awareness of the fear of not being a clear communicator do for me?

Stop your negative self-talk.

Thank you. What will stopping the negative self-talk do for me?

Allow you to relax and get on with your writing.

Thank you.

I've been doing NLP parts exercises for decades. I'm very used to talking to my parts and I usually get the answers very quickly. If you find that you have to wait for an answer, be patient and receptive to what is happening in you. Stay focused on the answer to the question, 'What will that do for me?' The part will give you an answer. Notice what unfolds. Usually, the answers will come in words. Sometimes you may find that a feeling, an image, or a sound may trigger a memory.

There are enormous benefits to be gained from listening to your own inner dialogue without judgement or approval. One advantage in working with your parts is the clarity you gain. Be open to hear the truth that emerges as each part communicates honestly. If you dialogue with the parts that are in conflict, please be willing to accept everything that is communicated even if you find some of it unpleasant.

Full awareness of what you express and what you are not expressing will show how you block your freedom to respond spontaneously with honesty and integrity. When you listen to the internal dialogue that blocks you from expressing yourself fully, you will gain many benefits that will sustain you on your quest for happiness.

If a client believes that the conflict is with someone or something outside themselves, they can do very little except complain or blame. I find it heart-warming to witness the transformation that happens in clients who take ownership of their emotions, issues and problems. The first step in the process is to get real. Clients need to deal with their own inner conflicts first before they can deal with the issues they have with their partner.

Once a client agrees to work on the conflicts that are in them, their issues become clearer, more explicit and detailed. When I coach clients who express negative feelings such as fear, frustration, resentment and anger, I nearly always get a shocked reaction if I say, 'That's beautiful. Your "negative feelings" are a gift that will point you in the direction of what you need to learn and where you need to grow.'

It's astonishing how quickly clients have a change of mind when they are open to receiving correct information. Simply changing a word or a thought can offer fresh insights that bring a change in basic assumptions and in perception. People tend to think negatively about lack of motivation until they discover that willpower is a limited resource.

How would it be for you to give yourself permission to express 'negative' emotions without any guilt? Some people wrongly believe that anger should not be expressed. A positive step you can take towards improving your self-awareness is to challenge your beliefs and assumptions. You may discover that with a new insight, you will feel empowered in situations where you once felt like a victim of misinformation.

What is your first reaction to hearing that 'negative feelings are a gift'? My first thought on being told this was disbelief. I was aware that love and fear were purported to be the two emotions that are behind every decision we make. It took me several months of personal work before I could get my mind around the idea that feelings such as frustration, resentment, irritation, anger and every feeling I thought of as undesirable could serve me well.

I refrained from suggesting that the concept of a 'negative gift' defied logic. I needed a detailed explanation as to why anyone would suggest this was an invitation to grow. I was blessed to have Fr Richard (Dick) McHugh, SJ, PhD as both my teacher and mentor. To my knowledge, Dick was the first PhD in the world in Neuro-Linguistic Programming (NLP). I could not have had a better role model to educate, guide and support me in removing the obstacles that got in the way of my being my best self.

'Negative emotions' cannot block your happiness without your full permission. Dick taught me that I should never assume that I understood what a person meant until I looked beyond their words and paid attention to the whole communication. There is more than one definition for the words 'irritation', 'frustration' and 'anger'. You will have your own unique way of experiencing the emotions you label with these words.

People who blame others for making them feel a certain way would do well to learn how they allow themselves to be affected by partners or colleagues. By giving others the power to trigger 'negative' emotions in them, they suffer emotional pain. The person they think of as the perpetrator is living rent-free in their mind and left unscathed while they suffer.

What do you say to yourself that stops you from using the wellsprings of unused talents that I feel confident are in you? It is not your 'negative' feelings but your programmed beliefs that block you from achieving your goals. Never allow the wrong belief that you can't achieve success block you. You achieve what you believe you can achieve.

If you want to feel happy and fulfilled, pay attention to the thoughts you focus on. Notice how you react to the positive and negative feelings that are in you. You are in control of your thoughts even though it doesn't always feel like that when you're miserable or depressed.

It's widely accepted that other people's expectations can be a powerful influence on whether you believe you will succeed or not. How empowered would you feel if you accepted that you have total control over your thoughts and the decisions you wish to make? Your ideas about what might happen in the future or of how your partner might react in any given situation are simply ideas. Your beliefs do not predict what will happen in reality.

To feel empowered and in control of your choices, you may want to question beliefs that limit your options:

- What if you dropped every belief that does not serve you well?
- What if you made the decision to make your needs as important as your partner's?
- What if you decided that your role in life is not to be a people-pleaser?

Coaches and counsellors are aware that when a person censors what they share, hides behind a mask or is reluctant or unable to say how they are feeling, it could be because they are not self-aware. They could find it difficult to find the language for sharing their feelings. It may also be that they are not in the habit of talking about personal issues.

Dealing with Internal Conflict

We have deeply ingrained ways of thinking and habits that may have served us well at one time but when they have outlived their usefulness, it's time to let them go. Both good and bad habits are etched into our neural pathways. Research on the ability of our brain cells to change, reorganise and create new neural pathways shows that it is possible to develop new behaviours in a matter of months.

Through performing a new behaviour with frequent repetition, the connections between the neurons in the brain change with the frequency of the performance.

The brain doesn't distinguish between good and bad habits, and it's difficult for the brain to unlearn. In her book, *Cleaning Up Your Mental Mess*, Dr Caroline Leaf emphasises that changing your brain is not a quick fix. She believes that it takes a minimum of sixty-three days to start seeing changes in your life. Sometimes, if there is severe trauma, it might even take longer.

Changing old habits may not be as difficult as you assume if you are willing to engage in introspection, and take the time to reflect on your personal beliefs and motives. Introspection involves self-examination with the intention of putting in the effort to make better choices. To understand how your past experiences have shaped the perceptions and interpretations you have of yourself, your partnership and the world, you will benefit from giving time to reflection and introspection.

You cannot have a sense of autonomy over your life while you hide what you feel from yourself or others. The fated day when Dick invited me to look on frustration as an invitation to grow started with the question, 'Is that what you think?' He was facilitating a Master Practitioner training programme in NLP in Ireland and I was a member of the training team.

To gain practical experience, the participants worked in

triads. Each person in the triad was given the opportunity to act as the coach, the client and the observer. I felt frustrated as I observed a participant who was acting as coach. She asked nosey questions to satisfy her curiosity and deflected from the client's agenda. I had to struggle to find something positive to say about her when I was talking to Dick about what I observed.

My honest assessment, which I failed to share, was that the participant who was acting as coach was not hearing the client. I could see no sign of improvement since she did her practitioner training the previous year. One part of me wanted to say this and another part of me didn't want to be negative. I was neither honest nor direct when Dick asked me the question, 'What do you really think?'

That day, I learned a monumental life lesson that I have never forgotten and want to share. If you and I avoid confronting difficult issues and dealing with painful emotions, they hold power over us. I acted in good faith. I had the positive intention of being kind because back then I believed the right thing to do was to be positive, look for the best, and focus on what a participant did well.

My programmed belief that I should always look for the best in people stopped me from giving an honest assessment. By censoring the truth, I was doing a disservice to myself, to the person I observed, and to the participant who was being coached.

On reflection, I found that the unfinished business I had with the participant blocked me from giving an honest report. The monumental life lesson is that unacknowledged and unexpressed feelings affect how we judge people and events.

Probing questions to ask when you are aware of internal

conflict are 'Is that really what I think?' or 'What am I avoiding talking about?' The gift when you feel uncomfortable in yourself and ill at ease is a challenge for you to grow. Notice if you feel uneasy but go along with a situation that challenges your sense of personal integrity.

If you feel uncomfortable about procrastinating but you still defer taking action, what is going on in you? If you have anxiety about a decision you've been putting off or a commitment you're not meeting, you might find it helpful to talk to the parts that are generating the conflict.

12

COMMUNICATION IS COMPLEX

A woman with a voice is by definition a strong woman. But the search to find that voice can be remarkably difficult.

MELINDA GATES

Partners with relationship problems are advised to communicate more if they want things to improve. Many who believe they are adhering to this advice report that talking to a partner often makes things worse rather than better. Poor communication is one of the most frequent issues that couples bring to coaching.

People think that communication should be simple because it just involves talking and listening. A lack of awareness about how we speak and how we listen is what makes effective communication complex. We can never eliminate misunderstandings but we can strive to minimise them.

How often has it happened that you said one thing and your partner heard something completely different? Does the following dialogue sound familiar? 'That's not what I said.' 'Well, it's what I heard.' 'That's not what I meant.' 'Well, what did you mean?'

Unfortunately, I will need to use technical terminology in this chapter, but I will do my best to keep jargon to a minimum. Frequently, I meet partners who think they are having a conversation about one thing but are talking at cross-purposes.

A basic tenet of Neuro-Linguistic Programming is that the language we use will both reflect and shape the way we think about the world around us. Our sensory awareness of the external world comes through what we see, hear, touch, taste and smell.

Sight, hearing and touch are the dominant senses involved in effective communication. My dominant sense, which is sight, is expressed in the language I use. If I had a conversation with someone I believed was making much ado about nothing, I might say something like 'I don't see why you're making such a fuss. It looks pretty straightforward to me.'

The visual language of 'seeing' and 'looking' would make perfect sense to another person whose sensory preference was visual. But a person who had an auditory or kinaesthetic preference would not understand what I meant. It's estimated that the dominant sense for sixty-five per cent of people is visual, for thirty per cent it's hearing, and five per cent it's kinaesthetic.

Visual language: 'I don't see why you're making such a fuss. It looks pretty straightforward to me.'

Auditory language: 'It sounds like you're making a lot of fuss. If you ask me, I'd say it's pretty straightforward.'

Kinaesthetic language: 'I don't grasp what everyone is getting so upset about. I feel it's pretty straightforward.'

Partners who have different sensory preferences may as well be speaking two different languages. Through learning and using the language of other people's sensory preferences, you can increase the chance that they will hear what you mean, not just what you say.

To become a more effective communicator, it's useful to have some knowledge of the concept of Preferred Thinking Styles (PTS) and sensory preferences. You may be amazed by the improvements that happen when you develop the ability to make accurate observations about why misunderstandings occur.

Untidiness is a very common issue that couples argue

about. It may seem like a very insignificant part of what makes a partnership work, but seemingly small things that cause annoyance and frustration matter. Here is an example of a brief conversation between married partners who have issues around the tidiness in their home.

Husband: This room looks so untidy.

Wife: I feel comfortable that we have that lived-in look in our home.

Husband: Imagine if anyone called by and saw it like this.

Wife: They would feel as relaxed and comfortable as I do.

Husband: How could anyone ignore this mess?

Wife: Our friends come to visit us not to see if the house is tidy.

It's obvious that this couple have no awareness of each other's sensory preferences. He wants his wife to see his point. She wants her husband to know how she feels. They wrongly assume they are having a conversation about the same thing, the state of their house. They are not communicating.

If you don't know what sensory preference your partner has, you will limit the effectiveness of your communication with him or her. The flawed belief that if you choose your words carefully people ought to understand what you mean needs to be shattered.

Someone can listen to every word you say, they may even repeat back the words you used; but if they have a different sensory preference to you, they won't have clarity about what you meant to communicate.

It seems most unfair to be accused of not listening when you know that you paid attention. A helpful tip I give clients is, please don't become defensive if your partner claims you didn't listen. A wise strategy for avoiding a row is to apologise. Say something like, 'I'm so sorry. What did you want me to hear that I missed?'

Partners who have problems communicating usually talk at cross-purposes. In the example above, the husband for whom sight was dominant looked on untidiness as reflecting badly on him. His wife, whose dominant sense was kinaesthetic, didn't see the mess, which is why she felt relaxed and comfortable.

It may take a couple of communication coaching sessions to learn how to notice a speaker's preferred thinking style. Let me give you an example of how matching sensory styles will work when one partner is visual and the other is kinaesthetic: 'When I look around and see the place untidy, it feels as uncomfortable for me as sitting on a hard chair is for you.' Introducing the kinaesthetic element, which is the wife's sensory language, would allow her to grasp the meaning of what the husband wanted to communicate.

An auditory person would not fully understand what that sentence meant. Here is a clearer communication for someone with an auditory sensory preference: 'I know you don't hear me when I say the room is untidy, but when I look around, the untidiness grates on me. The effect is like I'm listening to an orchestra that keeps going out of tune and hurting my ears.'

Does this explain how knowing your partner's sensory preference and preferred thinking style makes for good communication? People think in one of three representational systems. Internally, they will be generating visual images, or talking to themselves and hearing sounds, or having feelings.

One way you can confirm that this is true is by listening to the process words people use to describe their experiences. Process words are the verbs, adverbs and adjectives we use to reflect our sensory preferences and preferred thinking styles.

Visual thinkers say, 'I see what you mean', 'That looks good to me' or 'Please show me'. They think in pictures and visual images and tend to speak relatively fast. They react badly to interruptions. It's as if they are looking at a film and lose part of their picture. This makes it difficult to go back to the point before the interruption.

Auditory thinkers say, 'I hear what you say', 'That sounds good to me' or 'Please tell me'. They often talk to themselves, and will verbalise their thoughts to clarify what they are thinking.

People who have a kinaesthetic style of thinking are tactile. Often disrespectfully referred to as 'the touchy feeling types', they have a strong sense of body awareness. As they take time to check how they are feeling, they are often slow to answer.

Many issues that relate to miscommunication are poorly understood. I have decades of experience in communication coaching. Yet I frequently find it difficult to make sure that what I say is communicated clearly because there is always room for miscommunication to occur.

To hear the whole communication involves listening to the words, being aware of the tone of voice, eye contact, facial expression, gestures and body language. The context in which a conversation takes place is also important. If a client speaks very softly or there is external noise in the background, I might not hear every word.

Missing a word or a pause has the potential to completely change the meaning of what the speaker intended to communicate. If we are unable to give our full and undivided attention to the speaker, we could miss a slight hesitation, or overlook a pause, or fail to notice a gesture or a change in the tone of voice. All of these have an impact on what is heard and understood.

If someone sounds as if they are speaking to us in a

patronising tone, we hear and intuit the superior attitude. Most of us will switch off and stop listening if our perception is that we're being lectured. A person who is accused of not listening is likely to become defensive if they think the accusation is not justified. It may not be that the person failed to listen. They just did not hear what their partner intended to communicate.

Whenever we interact with others, we make assumptions based on intuition. If I'm having a conversation with you, your eye contact will show if you're paying attention. Intuitively, we know when someone is distracted and only half-listening.

If you are speaking to someone who is distracted, they may get the gist of what you said. Or they may totally misunderstand what you intended to communicate. If they are unaware of the importance of paying attention to facial expressions and body language, they may fail to sense your emotional reaction.

You may or may not be aware that you have criteria for how you want your partner to speak to you. If your unconscious expectations are not met, negative emotions may be triggered. For example, I've had clients confess that the tone of voice their partner used when they were fighting made them feel angry, ready to scream.

When you were a child, you may have heard an adult say, 'Don't you speak to me in that tone of voice.' That instruction makes it impossible for the child to please the adult. There is no good answer to 'How do you want me to speak to you?' A communication that places both people in an impossible situation is called a double bind.

Common double binds are demands for behaviour that can only be spontaneous. 'You should love me.' 'You ought to respect me.' 'You have to be more spontaneous.' In plain English, these one-sided demands have to do with a struggle for control.

A client who feels unable to address an issue, such as the way a partner speaks to them, may wrongly hold their partner responsible for their negative reactions. It's easier to blame others when we are emotionally hurt than to take full responsibility for what we were thinking and feeling that contributed to our negative reactions.

In situations such as this, I would probably invite a client to explore their motivation and positive intention. After a couple of probing questions, clients normally discover that they wanted their partner to change so that they would feel better. Bearing this in mind, I might ask a client, 'Is it possible that what you deem to be unacceptable and found upsetting has its origins in your unspoken expectations?'

Listen in to the conversation of a couple having a row. One partner says two words: 'Don't stop.' Is the meaning of 'Don't stop' self-evident for you? To assume it means to 'Stop' may be unwise. 'Don't stop' might sound like a request to desist but isn't it true that it could mean the exact opposite? It could also be an invitation to keep going.

What is said is not as important as the tone of voice in which it is said. If there is a pause after 'don't' and the speaker's tone of voice emphasised the word 'stop', you could probably interpret the message as stop and desist. If the two words are linked together and the words are spoken in a softer, gentler tone, 'Don't stop' might sound like an invitation to continue.

Clients are mostly unaware of how their voices sound when they speak. The tone of a voice affects how people interpret what they hear. This explains how the same sentence can be interpreted as sarcastic, judgemental, critical, demanding or authoritarian.

Someone who thinks that their partner spoke to them in a sarcastic tone of voice might wrongly assume their partner meant the opposite to what they said. The other partner may not be aware of this juxtaposition. It's another situation when two people believe they are having a conversation about one thing and they are talking at cross-purposes.

When you read a sentence, you observe how it is punctuated. A comma or two commas in the written word can totally alter the meaning of a sentence. A comma is easy to see. To notice a pause or hear the change in tonality, which emphasises or changes the meaning of what is communicated, is a learned skill that doesn't come naturally.

Please read the unpunctuated sentence, 'Woman without her man is nothing'. You understand every word in that sentence. Now look at what happens if I put in a single comma. The sentence reads, 'Woman without her man, is nothing'. If I put in two commas, the sentence reads 'Woman, without her, man is nothing' which conveys a very different message.

I trust this explains how little impact words have in communicating clearly. As you discovered in the 'Don't stop' example, two people can speak the same language, but misunderstandings arise because they attribute different meanings to what is heard.

Punctuation is to the eyes as pauses are to the ears.

With no bad intention, misunderstandings occur because at the most basic level, communication involves so much more than just talking and listening. When couples fight, they are in a highly emotional state and are likely to make assumptions about their partner's intentions. There are many other reasons for why a speaker may say one thing and the listener hears something completely different.

Another issue that can cause misunderstanding is that some words in the English language have the same spelling and pronunciation but several very different meanings. For example, the word 'trim' may refer to a body shape, removing unwanted parts or adorning a garment. Other words such as 'plane' and 'plain' have the same sound but a different spelling.

Many clients listen for the word meaning, which is a very basic level of listening. As children, we were told that God gave us two ears and one mouth because we should listen twice as much as we speak. Did anyone tell you that there are three elements to effective communication – talking, listening and hearing? To my mind, hearing is the most important skill in communication.

I have a core belief that our relationships are as good as our communication. Our communication is as good as our ability to listen and to hear with our ears and eyes. Let me elucidate on the concept of 'hearing with our ears and eyes'. There is a monumental difference between listening to the words and hearing the intended message.

If there are no abnormalities when a newborn baby is screened for hearing loss, there is very little attention paid to hearing. One result of this is the perception that listening and hearing are identical. They are not. In this context, I'm suggesting that we listen for the word meaning. To hear what the speaker means, we need to focus beyond the words and pick up on the eye contact, body language, facial expressions and non-verbal cues.

Only a tiny minority of people have the natural ability to listen so intently that they are aware of every pause, hesitation, and voice change. Pacing, how quickly or slowly someone speaks, the loudness or softness of the voice, the pitch and intensity, will have a bearing on how well we hear, interpret and connect with what a speaker says.

We communicate by what we say and by what we don't

Communication is Complex

say. If I send you a text and you don't reply, your silence is a non-verbal communication that is open to interpretation. We sense and make educated guesses about what silence means.

A most effective technique for a speaker seeking clarity is to say something like, 'I'm not sure I explained that well.' Effective communicators check that what they said was heard and understood. It's important to listen beyond the words to notice the non-verbal signals. The listener who seeks clarity might say, 'Can I check if this is what you meant, please?' or 'I'm not sure I understand. Can you say it another way, please?' Clients are normally very happy with the positive response they get as they put these techniques into practice.

Miscommunication can happen because of misunderstanding the spoken word. It can also happen because of poor listening skills. Many of us assume we're listening when we're only half-listening. If a part of you is focused on the word meaning and another part is thinking about what you're planning to say, you're half-listening.

Your partner may intuitively pick this up from your body language. Note that your intuition about the emotional content of the words you hear may be accurate or inaccurate. A break in eye contact or an interruption may signal to the speaker that the listener has a lack of interest in hearing their point of view.

If your partner misunderstands what you mean, the onus is on you to give a clearer message. Your partner cannot know what you do not tell them. It's worth repeating that hearing involves listening beyond the words. Hearing the whole communication involves paying attention to the words, tone of voice, eye contact, facial expression, gestures and body language.

If you intuit that your partner is unhappy with something you said, please seek clarification. Don't assume you're correct.

You might ask, can I check ...?

- It seems like you're upset.
- It appears that what I said sounded harsh.
- I sense that you feel uncomfortable.

Couples who have been together for a long time will often make inaccurate assumptions about what their partner thinks and feels. Some assume they have good communication because they talk about the practical things such as shopping, jobs and holiday plans. Discussing practical issues that affect the running of the home are only a tiny part of good communication.

I've worked with many partners who had a functional relationship but a sexless marriage. When sex is gone or very infrequent, partners lose the intimate connection that is necessary for an emotionally healthy, loving partnership. When asked, 'What do you do for fun?' some couldn't recall the last time they had fun together.

Many communication difficulties are historical in this sense. Issues occur early in the relationship when a couple are still madly in love. In those wonderful 'love is blind' days, it is easy to be agreeable, stay quiet and ignore minor frustrations. If one partner does something that is mildly irritating, the other ignores it or makes no comment.

To act as if you don't mind something that upsets you is unwise. Some partners pretend they enjoy something their partner likes when they don't. This deception can cause friction later. What is ignored and not dealt with often breeds resentment and can become toxic over time. To hide your feelings because you fear how your partner might react is effectively denying your own experience.

An issue that regularly comes up is that a client notices that their partner has gone silent and senses a feeling of coolness between them. When asked, 'What's wrong?' they are told, 'Nothing.' The dilemma for the person who senses this is not true is, should they doubt their intuition, suggest it's a lie or feel hurt that their partner is shutting them out?

A person who senses that their partner is holding something back will make assumptions about why they are not trusted with the truth. It would make such a difference if a partner said they needed time to process and they were not ready to have a conversation. 'I'm not ready to talk yet' is so much kinder than giving a partner the silent treatment. Misunderstandings are inevitable if a partner makes assumptions about what their partner refused to share. Mind-reading includes intuition as well as the guesses and assumptions partners make and treat as if they are facts.

'Intuition' is the ability to understand what is heard without having to use conscious reasoning. It is not as common as many people believe. A scenario I have come across on many occasions is a client who had a really hard day comes in from work. Their partner asks, 'How was your day?' The single word reply, 'Fine' closes down any conversation and shuts their partner out. Monosyllabic replies such as 'Nothing' or 'Fine' invite misunderstandings that will never be resolved without honest communication.

Some partners are very quick to shut down a topic or switch the subject when they feel uncomfortable. Avoiding what they are afraid may be a difficult conversation demonstrates a lack of sensitivity for a partner's need for sharing and connection.

I used to feel perplexed when I had a client tell me that a partner should have known they were not fine and done something to make them feel better. One client told me that one glance at her facial expression should have communicated that she needed tender loving care.

You might wonder why a person who said they were fine would expect that their partner should know what to do to make them feel better. Emotions are not based on logic but on a person's personal experience and expectations. The brain believes what we tell it and this has a powerful effect on how a person feels. I've also worked with clients who sensed that something was not right but when asked, their partner lied and claimed that nothing was wrong.

The emotional distress generated by unrealistic thinking is very real and is bound to put a strain on a partnership. I've worked with several clients who resented their partner for failing to meet needs that they admitted they had never expressed. A wise person said, 'Resentments are like drinking poison and waiting for the other person to die.'

Clients cannot always answer the question, 'How did you want your partner to respond?' Some people who sense that a partner is upset feel obliged to make things right but not knowing how to help, they remain silent and feel powerless. Others might answer, 'I don't know.' Or I might get a vague suggestion such as, 'I wanted him or her to do something, anything.' This is not helpful for either coach or client.

To empower a client to reflect at a deeper level I might ask, 'And if you did know?' and leave a long pause. Confident that the client has the answer, I remain silent and wait until the client replies. 'And if you did know?' is a trick question that challenges the brain to find an answer. On one occasion, there were twenty minutes of silence before the client shared a powerful insight.

Experiential insights that come from reflecting deeply have

the power to transform relationships. However, there are many reasons for why people avoid honest conversations that could potentially resolve difficulties. Fear of what might happen if they were open and honest keeps partners, who routinely have rows, stuck with their unresolved issues.

To communicate honestly requires self-knowledge, courage, and resilience. It takes a change in basic assumptions in thinking to drop the fear of what might happen; to allow yourself to be authentic and act with integrity. What could happen if you opened up to your partner? How do you feel when you think about having the freedom to ask for what you need?

Opening up may feel like too big a step to take just yet. The implications are huge. No holding back, no one-word answers, lying, or attempting to put a spin on the truth. Instead of deflecting or misdirecting when you want to avoid talking, you might say, 'I don't want to talk about it now. I'll let you know if and when I'm ready.'

Of course, there are parts of you that will be fearful of having the integrity to be authentic and say what you think. Clients are generally shocked at what they reveal to themselves when I ask probing questions about their unrealistic expectations. Powerful coaching questions can shock clients into taking personal responsibility for their mind-reading. Paying attention to their own internal dialogue will often give helpful insights.

I have good news and bad news for you. The good news is that you have the capability to be an effective communicator. The bad news is that much of your communication with your partner is at a basic level. The good news is communication techniques are easy to learn. The bad news is how unnatural they feel in the beginning when you start using new techniques.

As you change your style of communication, family members

may begin to ask, 'What's wrong with you? Why are you talking that way?' An approach that works well is to repeat the words back to them. 'Sounds like you think there is something wrong with how I'm talking.' Speak calmly and stay quiet.

What's beautiful about this communication technique is that it works. If you add 'sounds like', 'seems like' or 'appears that you think' to the exact words your partner says and then remain silent, your partner will feel heard. You're neither agreeing nor disagreeing, just repeating back the exact words they said. You must really listen to be able to do this accurately.

The saying, 'If you don't use it, you will lose it' applies to communication. Any skill that is not constantly used will deteriorate over time. It never goes away completely but the ease with which you use a skill will diminish the longer it remains unused.

I often ask partners, 'When did you last gaze lovingly at your partner?' I ask them to stand up, face each other, and look into each other's eyes without speaking for two minutes. For some partners, this takes a huge effort. Others who enjoy it are shocked at how long the exercise seems.

I'm guessing that in the first flush of romance, you naturally and effortlessly used all your senses to hear with your eyes, ears and hearts. The body language of a couple newly in love is unmistakable. It's obvious from the way they gaze adoringly into each other's eyes. It's visible in their posture as they lean in to each other. Totally focused in their own romantic bubble of happiness, they are oblivious to the outside world.

I'm confident that you and your partner have communication skills that you are not aware you possess. The heart-to-heart communication you once enjoyed can be enjoyed again, only this time it will take work and effort.

13

REFRAMING BELIEFS

You gain strength, courage and confidence by every experience in which you really stop to look fear in the face. You can say to yourself, 'I have lived through this horror. I can take the next thing that comes along.' You must do the thing you think you cannot do.

ELEANOR ROOSEVELT

Some couples who come for life coaching report that they have a good partnership that feels okay most of the time. Nothing serious is wrong with their relationship. They love each other and plan to stay together. They fight, but a comment that is often made is, 'So does everyone else.'

Other couples come because they have been through counselling. It didn't work for them. They would like to divorce, but financially are not able to do so. As one client said, 'Coach us on how to live together without killing each other'.

Many come through the recommendation of friends who transformed their partnership during relationship coaching. What all of these couples have in common is the desire for a more fulfilling partnership. Some are hurt and miserable and others want something they think is missing.

Couples with busy schedules will often drift into routine ways of relating. Minor disagreements that generate frustration and irritation occur almost daily for many partners. For some, these upsets are so normal they don't give them a thought. Others blame themselves for feeling dissatisfied when they should be grateful for what they have.

What a person ignores or lies about early in a relationship will usually come back to haunt them later. A small number of clients regret that they did nothing about seemingly minor issues they never talked about. Over time, issues that are ignored or avoided have the potential to grow into problems. Long-standing problems are difficult to resolve.

I love the story of the couple who went for counselling after they were married for three years. The counsellor asked the couple to tell each other one thing that would make a difference if it was changed. The husband's request to his wife was to stop cooking broccoli. After three years, he had reached the stage when he couldn't face another dinner served with broccoli – a vegetable he hated.

His wife blurted out, 'But I don't even like broccoli. I only cook it for you because you told me how much you loved it.' It transpired that the first meal his wife cooked, after they came back from their honeymoon, was served with broccoli. Not wanting to upset her, he lied and said the meal was delicious. The truth, when he told it, resolved that food issue.

Too often, people who don't want to offend their partner live with the consequences of a white lie. In this story, the truth set both people free. I once had a client who felt under enormous time pressure because she felt obliged to be at the beck and call of her family. Her belief was that she had to take her aunt shopping on a Wednesday and her mother shopping on a Friday.

After a coaching session, she plucked up the courage to ask if her aunt would be willing to change her shopping day to a Friday. Her aunt explained that she had wanted to talk about their shopping trips for some time but didn't know how to start the conversation.

The aunt's preference was to be independent and make her own arrangements on the days that suited her, but she didn't want to say anything for fear of upsetting her niece. The expectation that you will be disapproved of, won't be liked, or might be rejected if you fail to go along with what others expect of you is a universal experience.

If your programmed thinking has you believing that it is virtuous to make your partner's needs more important than your own, you need to change your thinking and reframe your beliefs. Your needs are as important as your partner's needs.

Honouring them is what the spiritual master Anthony de Mello, SJ called 'enlightened self-interest'. When you set out to meet your own needs, you get something; your partner gets something. You're both happy.

Did you learn that you should try to keep others happy? Do you make your partner's or your family's needs more important than your own? If you answer 'yes', it's likely that your self-care is not as good as it ought to be.

As children, many of us were told we must put others first and learn to control our negative emotions. As adults, some of us continue to be influenced by outdated fears around expressing 'unacceptable' emotions. Can you have an intact sense of self-worth if you fail to take care of your own needs?

The person who believes they must keep the peace at all costs has a positive intention that is probably motivated by fear; the fear of confrontation, the fear of retaliation, the fear of repercussions, and the fear of not being liked or loved. Depending on the circumstances and the size and status of who and what is involved, the fight, flight or freeze response kicks in. About eighty per cent of the decisions we make are motived by fear, not desire.

Feelings we ignore or deny don't go away. They remain alive and active within us. When emotions such as anger and fear are ignored or denied for long enough, they become suppressed. If you do not connect with how you feel emotionally, and if you are afraid to give expression to your anger, you lack the freedom to be who you are.

There is no doubt that ongoing unresolved issues drain the life and intimacy from a partnership. It's beautiful to hear clients say that although their partnership is not exactly what they desired or signed up for, there are many good parts they appreciate. Building on what works is a good place for coaching to begin.

Lack of intimacy is an issue that motivates couples to seek relationship coaching. It's common for a client to seek coaching on how to discuss sex with a partner when the couple behave more like friends than intimate lovers.

A failure to communicate is guaranteed to drive a wedge between partners. A frequent issue in couples coaching is that the sex is gone. Passion is a thing of the past. One partner's effort to have a serious conversation about this is brushed aside by the other. Fear is usually found behind a person's unwillingness to discuss an issue that is important for their partner.

'Fear' is an emotive word. Clients will frequently deny that they experience fear in their interactions with a partner. However, when I define 'fear' as an uncertain reaction to a threat, such as the danger of sparking a row, the anguish at growing apart or the emotional outcome of a partner's refusal to engage in a serious conversation, clients usually accept the appropriateness of the word.

No two people react in the same way to the same event. Some partners feel threatened by just the thought of being asked to engage in an embarrassing conversation. A person may deflect or gently brush their partner's request aside. If the partner persists, they may show signs of impatience and finally, they may react with an angry outburst.

Fear, anger and resentment are very closely connected emotions. In theory, we have choices about how we respond emotionally, but we are not always in control. I witnessed a client erupt in an explosive, angry outburst when his partner's demand for an explanation goaded him into reacting.

In that situation, the fear that the perceived threat elicited in him triggered a defensive eruption of anger. Ashamed for yelling at his partner, he immediately apologised profusely to us both. I accepted his apology as sincere. His partner appeared gracious when she accepted his apology. Then she turned to me and said, 'Do you see what I have to put up with?'

Some people who are addicted to drama will deliberately manipulate situations to give themselves the negative feelings they desire. Couples know how to push each other's buttons. My guess was the client wanted to show up her partner in a bad light. I surmised that she knew what to expect when she goaded him and he gave her exactly what she wanted.

What prevents you from saying the things you would like to say and from doing the things you would like to do? You might use words such as shyness, anxiety, reluctance, or hesitation. I use the word 'fear'. Whatever word you use when you describe how you stop yourself from acting spontaneously is right for you.

If you find it difficult to articulate your feelings, if you do your best to ignore emotional hurt and pay little attention to small frustrations, fear is alive and active in you, whether you are aware of it or not. Fear makes us feel vulnerable, and not in control. A way to subconsciously deal with unexpressed feelings of fear is to move into anger.

Let's say you feel angry because you want something you're not getting. Do you express that anger in a healthy way or do you ignore it? Feelings you ignore or deny don't dissolve and disappear, they remain alive in you. Have you witnessed someone who was radiating rage and said, 'I'm not angry'? Everyone but the person could see the repressed anger that the person genuinely did not feel. They were numb to their own emotions.

People who numb themselves to fear are likely to have disconnected from healthy feelings of anger. If they are out of touch with their emotional state, the fear, anger and resentment they fail to express in an appropriate and respectful way will become toxic and poison their relationships.

If fear and anger are shut down or ignored for long enough, they become suppressed. When a person finds it difficult to express feelings in a healthy way, their emotions will build up. Over time, the suppressed emotions become repressed. When this happens, the feelings are in the person but the person does not experience them.

If their anger is triggered, they can explode in an outburst of aggression, hostility, blame, critical judgements or vindictiveness. The person who has a pattern of reacting with an over-the-top outburst of anger followed by a grovelling apology has not made a sincere effort to change their behaviour. The apology of a person who fails to make a genuine effort to change unacceptable behaviour is worthless.

Honest and open communication is crucial for an emotionally healthy partnership. When a feuding couple take an honest look at why they fight, they will usually find that fear and hurt are their triggers for resentment and anger. Resentment develops when needs are denied or ignored. It's natural to fear and resent a partner's outbursts of anger.

Partners who are trapped in a vicious cycle of dysfunctional behaviour need individual sessions before a coach can work with them as a couple. The focus in counselling is on healing emotional pain by looking at how a client's past history affects their current behaviour. The focus in coaching is on empowering partners to find strategies that will work now and in the future.

Occasionally, I have had to challenge a client about unacceptable behaviour. If a coach models how to communicate honestly and respectfully when confronting inappropriate behaviour, the client experiences the benefits of receiving honest feedback. For example, the sentence 'I felt intimidated when you yell; please do not shout' gives a clear message in a non-judgemental way.

Educating clients to work with their thoughts, and to identify and express their feelings, is an important step on the quest for happiness. Once couples recognise and acknowledge their role in generating conflict situations, they are ready to be introduced to the power of reframing, which is one of the most useful coaching tools.

Couples who row a lot usually lack the communication skills to have a respectful conversation. Poor communication is among the most common reason for partners splitting up. Can you sustain a loving relationship with a partner who will not converse with you? Are you surprised that many clients reply 'yes' to this question?

Clients tend to get uneasy when I ask, 'Can you love a partner that you do not trust to respect you?' I explain that 'getting to the truth demands total honesty from you, no fudging, white lies or massaging of the truth'. I ask, 'May I hold the mirror up to shine a light on what I see and hear?' This is a powerful tool to illustrate how partners are responsible for setting up the patterns in their relationship that create discontent.

In my experience, the recipe for estrangement is a failure to communicate. I understand the partner who accepts being a golf-widow or puts up with the long hours a partner works. Their partnership works if they enjoy the companionship they share when they are together. What is hard for me to understand is the decision of a person who chooses to feel miserable, unhappy and scared with a partner because they fear living on their own.

I'm sensitive to the impact words have to cause hurt and distress. This is why I put a lot of thought into the impact that words such as 'fear', 'anger' and 'abuse' will have on clients before I use them. I have a very simple definition of the word 'abuse': Any intentional action that causes emotional or physical harm to another is abusive.

It's wrongly believed that there is no abuse if there is no domestic violence. That is setting the bar very low indeed. 'Abuse' is an emotive word, which I am not afraid to use with clients who need a reality check. The question 'I'm wondering if you consider that abusive behaviour?' will usually get an outraged denial. Would you say that a client who lives with uncertainty, fearful of their partner's next angry outburst is in an abusive relationship? Would you say the same about a person who nags and goads their partner until they get an angry reaction?

Every couple I have coached unconsciously engaged in patterns of behaviour that were not emotionally healthy. Clients are often disappointed when I tell them, 'Leave your partner out of this for now. I don't need to hear a detailed account of what happened. I want to work with you in present moment freshness.'

Regardless of what the presenting issue is in a session, my coaching style is to guide every client to connect with their thoughts and take ownership of their feelings. Some things I might say after the client sets the agenda for the session are:

- How are you right now?
- Stay with what is happening.

- Don't push the feeling down.
- What are you thinking?
- Give me your first uncensored thought.
- Is there any other way of looking at or seeing that?

Self-knowledge is priceless. It has everything to do with empowering a client to achieve their goals. People who can deal with fraught situations are so much better when they are managing their emotions well. When clients have rapport with their coach, when they feel safe enough to connect with the deeper feelings they hold inside, most will become aware of the role that unrecognised fears played throughout their lives.

Reframing is one of the best tools I know for managing your emotions well. The goal in reframing unhelpful beliefs is to look at the same facts from different perspectives. In simpler terms, reframing is an invitation to change how you are looking at things.

This doesn't involve looking through rose-tinted spectacles, denying reality or deluding oneself with positive psycho-babble. It's a practical and logical tool for managing your emotions and going after the results you want. It's the gateway to dipping into the wellsprings of unused talents and untapped potential that were formerly blocked by unnamed fears.

Is there any logic to feeling annoyed or angry if you are caught in a heavy shower without an umbrella? It's understandable that a person would have negative feelings if they don't like getting wet. Many might say, such negative reactions are natural, but are they? To invite a client to reframe in this context, I might ask:

- Do you get any practical benefit from reacting negatively?
- Is there any other way of looking at the situation?

- How would you feel if you made the choice to look at it from that fresh perspective?

When we make a choice to look at a situation from one perspective, we also make the choice to avoid looking from other perspectives. Rain is rain. Whether you like it or not is a choice. You could if you choose enjoy the rain, get very wet, and splash through puddles. What would this choice do for you? Could it take you out of your mind and bring you to an enjoyable sensory experience?

I'm not saying that changing behaviour patterns is easy. It's not. It's challenging and involves persistent and determined effort. When your narrative is 'I must' your belief is that you don't have a choice. In most situations, this is not true. You may not control the situation you are in, but you always have choices about how you respond.

A part of you will resent any perceived demand that you feel under pressure to meet. Any decision you make that is motivated by fear puts you in the role of victim. This will make you feel less capable than you are, which will result in diminished self-esteem, eroded confidence and a damaged sense of self-worth.

Everything that is happening in your life today is because of the past choices you made. Many of us make choices unconsciously. Therefore, we don't consider them choices, and yet they are. You have a choice if someone insults you. Think about this, you could choose to be insulted or you could decide not to be offended.

Whether you are aware of it or not, words elicit a real emotional response in you. The physical sensations people experience when they fear or anticipate a future event are very alike. The person who labels feelings of tension and butterflies in their stomach as feeling excited and ready, will have a positive if mildly uneasy experience.

The person who fears something bad may occur could also experience tension and butterflies. If such a negative but equally valid experience was reframed as a false expectation appearing real, it could make for a more enjoyable experience. Everyone has the power to reframe their thoughts about any experience. It is astonishing how simply choosing a different way of wording what you say to yourself can change your emotional state.

Finding the language to talk about emotions is a challenge. Anger is a complex emotion that is often seen as a harmful and undesirable feeling. 'A strong feeling of annoyance, displeasure or hostility' may be a dictionary definition of unhealthy anger, but those words overlook the positive energy that healthy anger generates.

I was invited to reframe my beliefs about anger decades ago when I was doing the Master Practitioner in Neuro-Linguistic Programming (NLP) training. The trainer valued anger as a healthy emotion. He invited us to think of anger as a positive, connecting, energising emotion that empowered us to take action.

You may or may not relate to the concepts of fear and anger as I have described them. If the words 'fear' and 'anger' do not appropriately reflect your experience, you may find it more beneficial to pay attention to the physical sensations in your body. A feeling of unease or physical discomfort may be the signal that alerts you to the wisdom of reflecting on how you motivate yourself to react.

We make choices all the time. Some are conscious and considered, and some less so. All choices have consequences. In my experience working with couples who come for relationship coaching, the presenting issues are rarely the issue they need to work on to come up with a win/win solution.

Partners are jointly responsible for the current state of their partnership. If everything is not how a couple wants it to be, it's because their attitudes, their thinking and their emotions need to be challenged. It may be hard to get one's head around the idea that each person has chosen the thoughts, feelings and behaviours that generated the pain they suffer.

When I work with partners who are in conflict, there is always one person, and sometimes two, who believes that if they could only get their partner to modify their behaviour, they would live happily ever after. Thinking that one's unhappiness, frustration, annoyance, whatever emotive words are used, are the result of one's partner's deeds is putting responsibility on the wrong person. At first, couples find it difficult to accept that each person is responsible for their own happiness.

Take for example the perennial problem when two partners have different standards of tidiness. Jill feels angry because Jack never cleans up after himself. She complains that she is tired asking him to put the mugs in the dishwasher, to put his dirty clothes in the linen basket, and to stop leaving wet towels in the bathroom. Jack is unhappy about Jill's 'one use, one wash' philosophy.

Jack accepts that he is not the tidiest of people. He feels he is protecting the environment when he leaves wet towels to dry on the radiator in the bathroom. He complains that Jill's nagging puts him off making any effort. Untidiness is one of the issues they fight about all the time. Both of them are aware that there is a pattern to their rows.

Sometimes they start when Jill is in a bad mood and she complains about having to do something that Jack has left undone. Other times Jack has tried to be tidy for a couple of days. Jill doesn't appear to notice. Discouraged that his efforts are not appreciated, he drifts back to his old ways.

Their unresolved issues make for a terrible atmosphere. Jack deflects by accusing Jill of nagging, which annoys her even more. She feels peeved that he makes her so angry. Her belief is that no one should be thanked for tidying their own belongings. Jill believed that all her issues would be resolved if Jack's untidiness could be fixed. Jack had two issues to be resolved, his inability to live up to Jill's standards and her lack of appreciation for his efforts.

Jill and Jack have expectations of each other that are not being met. Jill wants Jack to keep their home tidy and to stop accusing her of nagging. Jack wants the efforts he makes to please Jill, to be appreciated and affirmed. Each believes that what they want the other to do is reasonable and should be achievable.

Many clients have clarity about what they desire but some admit they are unclear about what they want. It's surprising how frequently a client answers 'I don't know' to the question, 'If you don't want that, what specifically do you really want?' A person who doesn't know what they want will never be happy.

Some people unconsciously limit their life choices because of the need to feel protected and safe from imagined scenarios that they create for themselves. Fear of what could go wrong if they take a risk makes people cautious.

As we've covered in Chapter 11, the amygdala is a small organ in the middle of the brain. It alerts our nervous system when we instinctively sense danger and triggers the body's fear response. Even a threat to self-esteem will trigger this response. The brain does not distinguish between what is a real and what is a perceived danger.

Feeling afraid is a healthy emotional response. It is necessary to be conscious of fear when we believe that we are not safe and need to protect ourselves from a perceived threat. For clarity, I suggest we think of fear as being on a spectrum.

At its lowest level, there is a sense of unease if we are wondering, 'Should I stay silent or say something?' At the upper level of the spectrum, I'd put the fear that a partner might inflict physical violence.

The limitations of using the same word to describe the sense of uneasiness and anxiety experienced when feeling uncomfortable in a social situation as well as the emotional distress experienced during an angry, abusive shouting match or a domestic violence situation is obvious.

With improved communication skills, partners can overcome the limitations they put on their own capabilities. An effective technique is to have a couple sit facing each other. Each person makes a list of sentences beginning with the words 'I can't'. For example:

- I can't say that to my partner.
- I can't ask to defer our date because I want to go to the football match.
- I can't say how much I paid for the shoes.

Taking about three minutes, the couple tell each other the assumptions they made, starting each sentence with 'I guess you would'. It's interesting for each person to find out to what extent they are correct about what they assume about their partner's reaction and to what extent they are wrong.

Most clients are pleasantly surprised at how different their lives look when they make the decision to reframe their beliefs. Trust me, you will find endless opportunities to see how looking at everyday situations from different perspectives will multiply your choices and change your perspectives.

Reframing is a useful tool for taking back control and managing your emotional state well. The theory in NLP is that every person has the resources they need to make any desired change. Could you feel happier, less dissatisfied, more content and at peace in yourself if you reframed some of the limiting beliefs you hold? What if you looked on fear and anger as healthy emotions, which play an important role on the path to finding true happiness?

Mark Twain's character Tom Sawyer was assigned the task of painting a fence but he wanted to go swimming with his friends. His creativity came to the fore when he reframed the work as enormous fun. When his friends came along, they had to pay him to have a turn at painting the fence. When his aunt looked out, a richer Tom was happily reclining on the grass.

The ability to reframe an experience in a new way offers a fresh perspective and new possibilities. Pete and Angie were crippled with credit card debt and worried that their washing machine kept breaking down. Angie was stressed they couldn't afford to buy a replacement. It upset her that Pete didn't seem to care about how worried she felt.

The emotional impact of worrying about what might happen in the future was making Angie depressed. Invited to brainstorm about what they could do if the worst came to the worst, Angie came up with the suggestion that they could wash the clothes in the sink. Pete suggested they could take the washing to a launderette and he would change his clothes less often.

By looking at their situation from a different perspective, they came up with practical solutions that could work. Reframing didn't change the fact they were struggling, but it demonstrated that they had choices. They were able to come up with strategies for making the best of a bad situation.

The presenting issue for Angie was financial stress. She needed Pete to show he cared about her feelings. Pete flinched when Angie said he didn't care, but he didn't comment. Afraid of how she would react, he didn't tell her he was so worried that he had sourced a launderette. It was heartwarming to see Angie reach out to take his hand when he told me this.

I explained to Pete that his partner can't know what he doesn't tell her. I said to Angie, 'Isn't it beautiful that Pete was empathic and concerned about how you might react? He must care for you very much.' 'I never thought about it like that,' she replied.

Coaching a couple to understand how misunderstandings occur because of assumptions or lack of communication is always satisfying. When Pete admitted that he was worried, Angie was able to view their situation from a different perspective. The problems remained but with a changed attitude, they found possible ways to cope.

Most of the issues that create conflict between partners are never resolved. But every couple can learn how to compromise, agree to differ, and reframe how they think and communicate.

14

KNOW YOURSELF

True love is not a feeling by which we are overwhelmed. It is a committed, thoughtful decision.

M. SCOTT PECK, *THE ROAD LESS TRAVELLED*

Charles Horton Cooley, an American sociologist at the start of the twentieth century, said: 'I am not who you think I am; I am not who I think I am; I am who I think you think I am.' I love this quotation because it so beautifully illustrates that we live in a perception of a perception of ourselves.

I so identify with the statement, 'I am not who you think I am.' My husband died the day after our forty-fourth wedding anniversary. I had to fill in forms after his death that labelled me as 'the surviving spouse or widow'. This is not how I see myself. Who I am cannot be altered by a change in my marital status or profession or life circumstances. It may however change how others think of me and of how I behaved as I figured out how to be single.

Deepak Chopra said, 'Everything that is happening at this moment is a result of the choices you've made in the past.' The experiences you built up throughout life have helped to shape the person you are today. Factors that contributed to who you are today include your family upbringing, life experiences, education and genetics.

What you believe about yourself has an impact on how you react and present yourself in different situations today. Your personal beliefs are shaped by your life experiences, particularly during childhood and adolescence. The feedback you received from your parents, extended family, teachers and others have all contributed to your beliefs about who you are and what is important to you.

Your self-image reflects the social masks you wear and the roles you play. Perhaps you think of yourself as fashion- conscious or as someone who has certain traits. You might describe yourself as being shy or outgoing, academic or athletic, energetic or easy-going.

These are facets of your personality.

You may have a career as a teacher, a doctor, a life coach, or a cleaner. Your career is what you do, not who you are. The more self-awareness and understanding you have of your own thoughts, feelings, and behaviours, the closer you are to finding your authentic self.

In the aftermath of a significant event such as divorce, changing career, death of a partner, redundancy or retirement, it's natural to struggle with the age-old question, 'Who am I now?' This presumes that there might be a plausible answer, as if your identity could – or should – be reduced to a fixed description. There is no one answer because life is constantly changing.

Being 'who you are' means embracing your values, beliefs, personality, and individuality. It involves understanding and accepting yourself exactly as you are, not as you would like to be. Self-acceptance empowers you to live authentically with a beautiful sense of serenity and freedom.

People who set out to find themselves are usually struggling with their core sense of self and grasping for a concrete answer. At different stages in your life, you have probably asked such philosophical questions as:

Know Yourself

- What really matters to me?
- Where do I fit in?
- What do I want to do with the rest of my life?

All of us play multiple roles in life, among them child, partner, friend, colleague, neighbour, and acquaintance. Who you really are is the person underneath the roles you play and the masks you wear. Who you are is 'you' with your feelings, attitudes and values intact. What makes this challenging for 'you' is that you show different parts of yourself to family, friends and acquaintances.

The title of a book that had a huge impact on me when I was starting out on my own quest for happiness was was written by John Powell, an American Jesuit priest. It was called *Will the Real Me Please Stand Up?* I have little memory now of the contents of the book. What I have never forgotten is the shock of my realisation when I read the title. 'The real me' couldn't stand up because I had no clue as to who I was.

Only you can get to the heart of who you are. No one else in the world has your unique set of experiences. Your relationship with yourself is forever changing. You will have many different answers to questions such as 'Who are you?' and 'What makes you happy?' Happiness is not a static emotion. It's fleeting and unstable.

At one time, being with your partner made you blissfully happy, but for how long did your blissful state last? The uncomfortable truth that people prefer to ignore is how brief and fleeting those heightened experiences of bliss and happiness are.

Partners look back on their early days together with great pleasure. Setting up home when you are madly in love and have no real responsibilities is wonderful. To learn how to live together in ways that suit both people soon brings up differences.

Disagreements about how chores are divided, whether to watch soaps or sports, or how to deal with finances are rarely fully resolved.

The most effective communication skills in the world cannot guarantee an unruffled partnership. Even the best-matched, happiest partners are bound to have disagreements dealing with practical matters. Many partners never sort their differences out. They never get to the root of their problems because their programmed beliefs, about how things should be, block their happiness.

Some people ignore problems in the sense that they fail to make a genuine effort to deal with them together. Others argue and fight rather than attempt to find a workable solution.

If you genuinely want to know why you feel disillusioned and unhappy with your partner, I'll tell you, but you won't like my answer. It's because your partner is not giving you exactly what you want. You are programmed to believe that getting what you want and avoiding what you don't want will bring you happiness. It won't.

Can you recall a time when you felt overwhelmed with happiness? Did those good feelings come from something inside of you or were they triggered by something external? Was it by your partner or some celebration? Having your desires met, which is an external source of happiness, gives you a moment of happiness, that's all. You experience a temporary good feeling that gives you respite from the negative feelings that block your happiness.

Emotions are volatile. A person can go from feeling down in the dumps to ecstatic in an instant. This is why we say there is no such thing as a tired lottery winner. Someone may feel so exhausted that they can barely keep their eyes open. Their

Know Yourself

numbers came up. They have won the lottery. In a split second, they are fully energised, excited and overflowing with happiness.

How does this apply to you? Have you ever driven on a motorway when the car in front of you was driving at least 10 km under the speed limit? Were you so annoyed and frustrated that you shouted at the driver to drive faster, stop slowing you down? I've encouraged you to express how you feel and to work at having an open, non-judgemental mind.

Now, I'm inviting you to get real and to remove the obstacles you put in your own path that block your happiness. Do you think it's natural to be upset if you're in a hurry and someone slows you down? Many clients have a perception that they were not bothered before they were delayed. Think carefully before answering. Were you really fine before this happened?'

There is no logic to upsetting yourself with negative feelings when your effort to control the speed of other motorists is not successful. For what reason would you shout at or speak to a driver who couldn't hear you? Isn't it because you were not getting what you wanted? The slow driver has no responsibility for the negative feelings you generated in yourself. You wanted the person to drive faster and when they didn't, you upset yourself.

We unconsciously do illogical things because of our programming. The programmed brain makes demands. When they are not met, the conditioned response is to react with a negative feeling. You were programmed to believe that when you have upset feelings, someone or something outside yourself is to blame. As you work on getting to know yourself better, you will learn that this is a flawed belief.

Pavlov was famous for his experiments with dogs. He demonstrated that if you give a dog something to eat every time you ring a bell, soon the dog begins to salivate when you ring the bell. The dogs developed conditioned reflexes to the stimulus of the sound of the bell.

Even though we can make choices, most of us have become a mass of conditioned reflexes. Dependent on past experience, training and learning, we frequently react without thinking. A stimulus for us can be any person, place, event or thing that triggers a physical or behavioural reaction. In humans, there is a space between the stimulus and the response. In that space, we can choose to change how we react to the stimuli that previously triggered negative reactions.

Choosing to change our conditioned reactions takes time, patience, and self-awareness. In this context, self-awareness is the ability to focus on oneself and to be aware of how your thoughts generate your emotions and actions.

Your thoughts are whatever you want them to be. If you are in emotional pain, it is because you choose to focus on thoughts that disturb and bother you. You can reframe those thoughts, you can dwell on them, or you can let them go. The choice is yours.

You will need to identify the triggers that stimulate a conditioned response in you. If a thought generates a painful emotion, you don't have to dwell on the thought. If you wish, you can change it to another thought.

- You can picture anything you want in your mind.
- The picture can be any size and colour you want.
- Picture a seaside on a sunny day.
- Make the image life size.
- See the people on the beach.
- Hear children laughing.
- Feel the heat of the sun and watch the tide coming in.

Does the mind picture look, sound and feel real to you even though the seascape doesn't exist? Self-awareness is the key to knowing yourself. How do you develop self-awareness? You learn to watch what comes up inside of you. Connect what you are thinking with how you are feeling.

When you reflect on this, doesn't it seem simple and logical? Your thoughts have the same validity as the picture. They exist in your mind and not in reality. I want you to be fully aware of what is happening in you as you read the next paragraph.

To know yourself means to notice what is going on inside of you all the time. If you feel bitter, angry or frustrated, you have real feelings in response to thoughts that you made up. What was your first uncensored thought? Don't judge. What was the emotion and physical feeling that accompanied that thought?

When you recognise you feel upset, you have a choice. In the nanosecond when you are aware of what is happening in you, you can make a decision. You can do what you have always done or you can try something new. Your growth and the freedom to be truly who you are lies in making better choices.

What makes life difficult, relationships painful and situations unbearable is your programming. Distress happens when your mind is in the past, going over past wrongs, or in the future, catastrophising about things that might never happen. Getting rid of the obstacles to happiness involves living in the present and thinking in new ways.

You can only live one moment at a time. Both the past and the future are unreal in the sense that they don't exist in present, ongoing reality. The present moment is never intolerable. What causes upset is to be physically here when your mind is in the past or in the future. I'm making an educated guess that you will learn that for much of the time, you are living in your head.

A beautiful example that everyone can relate to is that when you're peeling the orange, you're eating the fruit. Your hands are taking the rind off, but your mind is elsewhere. When you're eating the orange, you don't taste it because your mind has moved on to something else. The body is there physically, but you are not present.

I will often use an orange to demonstrate how to get out of the head and into the senses. If I'm facilitating a larger group, I'll use dried fruit such as a raisin or sultana to offer the same experience.

The instructions for eating the orange are simple:

- Be aware of holding the fruit in your hand.
- Smell the fruit before you start to peel it.
- Notice the weight and the colour.
- Focus on what your hands are doing.
- Feel how the peel is on your fingers and your nails.
- Enjoy the aroma of the fruit.
- Bring the orange to your lips.
- Feel the saliva come into your mouth.
- Now taste the fruit.

The instructions for eating the dried fruit are to use all your senses as you put the fruit in your mouth:

- Focus on the sensations of bringing the fruit to your mouth.
- Feel the sensations of having it in your mouth.
- Explore it with your tongue.
- Notice the saliva coming into your mouth.
- Allow yourself to taste it, but don't chew it just yet.
- Now allow yourself to chew the raisin.

- Very consciously, bite the fruit and notice what happens.

People who do these exercises for the first time will usually exclaim that they never, ever tasted an orange or dried fruit before. I find this a beautiful way to introduce clients to the experience of how to be you, to be here, and to be present in the now.

A very simple exercise to get out of your head and live in the present is to verbalise what you are doing as you do it. In the beginning, it will take a little effort because it will slow you down. The beauty of experiential learning for clients is they feel the difference in themselves. Practical and simple awareness exercises like these give immediate benefits. They are enjoyable, relaxing and show how good it feels to be fully present, to get out of your head and come to your senses.

Some clients find it hard to accept that reacting negatively is a choice. They refuse to accept that choices that are unconsciously made are choices, but truly they are. Reactions can be automatically triggered, but as clients become aware of where their reactions come from, their decision-making improves.

The truth is that all desires and yearning generate emotional disturbance. Sadly, most of what we conceive of as true is mostly shaped in our minds. Taking responsibility for your own happiness is a monumental challenge. To accept that if you're unhappy it's because your partner is not giving you what you want goes against what was modelled and taught to you.

When you were very much in love with your partner, I'm guessing that you both were very much in agreement most of the time. Early love is like a powerful drug and under its influence, you felt amazing, sexy, beautiful and wonderful. What happened was your partner stimulated positive feelings that were already in you.

It was not your partner but your changed thinking, the

different perception you had of yourself, that generated all those wonderful feelings. The happiness and love you felt were generated internally. The unconditional love and acceptance that made you feel so happy were stimulated by your partner, but they were already inside of you. Your partner didn't make you feel all those wonderful feelings. Something was triggered in you that allowed you to connect with your own best self.

In the early stages of a romantic relationship, the level of rapport may feel so intoxicating that lovers are in danger of becoming blind to each other's flaws and deficiencies. Rapport is an essential part of building trust and making an emotional connection. The likelihood of making bad decisions when we are overly influenced by this beautiful heart connection is quite high.

A sense of deep connection is beautiful when you and your partner are first in love. The ability to demonstrate that you trust each other, understand how each other feels, communicate well and respect what the other thinks suggests that you enjoy good rapport, but this level of intense connection rarely lasts.

Love and happiness evolve and changes all the time. Let's say a couple go out for a meal to celebrate an anniversary. Everything feels perfect. The food is delicious, the ambience delightful, and the service is excellent. They have such a wonderful experience that they decide they will celebrate their anniversary in that venue the following year.

They go there for their next anniversary but it is not the same. Compared to the first time they were in the restaurant, nothing is as wonderful. Their expectations could not be met because they were comparing the present to a memory they had embellished. Can you savour the food you are eating if you are in your head, making comparisons with what you ate a year ago?

When the romantic stage of a relationship wanes, reality

sets in. The rose-tinted spectacles come off and your partner begins to do little things you find annoying. Something simple, such as how your partner squeezes toothpaste out of the tube or fails to put the cap back on it, can become an issue.

In the overall scheme of things, one might think it is silly to upset yourself over toothpaste. There is a part of you that recognises that the upset is not about the need to control your partner. Nor is it about a tube of toothpaste. The stimulus for the upset is the belief that if my partner truly loved me, they would do what I want them to do.

When you do something freely, for the joy or satisfaction it brings, that is when you are authentically yourself. Are you aware of your motivation when you do something with the desire to please your partner? Are you motivated by love or fear?

The spiritual masters tell us that there are only two emotions, love and fear. What is not motivated by love is motivated by fear. What is your reaction as you read this? Are you aware of where that reaction is coming from? If you're not, can you claim to know yourself?

The fear of being yourself is a fear of being judged. People who are afraid to be themselves will avoid asking for what makes them happy or try to indirectly get what they want. They may also feel the need to be constantly agreeable and avoid stating a contrary opinion, even if they disagree.

Think of the last time you were annoyed with your partner and said nothing. Search for the fear underneath your silence. Were you constrained by forces within you of which you had no awareness? Has it ever struck you that there isn't an attitude, a thought or an emotion you have that has not come from someone else?

You feel strongly about how your partner should do things.

You assume it is you who has these feelings, but is it really? When you answer the question, 'Is it you or is it your programming that caused your upset feelings?' you will discover the truth of what I'm saying.

Self-awareness incorporates self-observation, self-knowledge, and the ability to look inwards to connect the thoughts and feelings that influence your emotional state. To fully understand and accept the truth in the statement, 'I am who I think you think I am' you will need to move from your head to connect with your heart.

The only way I know to listen with your heart is through self-awareness. Learn to pay attention to why you are doing what you are doing. Self-knowledge is to understand and accept why you do what you do without approval or judgement.

How would you feel if you were happy, if you felt free to be you? Would your heart be full to overflowing? Would you be without a care in the world? Use whatever words and descriptions you like for the good feelings that allow you to feel energised and alive. For the moment, I want you to focus solely on yourself and name for yourself the good feelings I call 'happiness'.

I can't tell you what happiness is, that is something that you will have to figure out for yourself. I can tell you that if you're serious in your quest for happiness, you will need to embrace both positive and negative emotions. Did anyone ever tell you that many of our so-called 'negative emotions' are essential for your personal growth and development?

When you struggled with challenging experiences, overcame difficulties and survived, did you learn important life lessons? I'm confident that every time you found the courage and the inner resources to move on from a painful experience, you became a stronger person.

Clients are surprised when I ask them to name the strengths they discovered that empowered them to cope from childhood to the present day. Each of us has something powerful inside, an inner voice, that motivates us to keep going. In all our lives, there were times when we felt we were falling apart. We managed to pick up the pieces, put ourselves back together again and got on with life.

Those are the occasions that allow one's sense of self-esteem and self-worth to grow and develop. The tragedy is that so few of us recognise or appreciate this. It is never too late to connect with the good feelings that are in you because of your past endeavours. Naming those strengths will allow you to stop feeling afraid to connect with the positive feelings of happiness, achievement and success that are rightly yours.

Your mind is so connected to your heart that what your mind is thinking, your heart is feeling. I don't doubt that you will find there are fears in you that stop you from making the decision to feel happy, fulfilled, at peace and comfortable in your own skin:

- What is the worst thing that could happen if you had the freedom to be authentically yourself?
- What is the best thing that could happen if you had the freedom to be authentically yourself?

If you aren't sure who you are, you will always have a fear that others will discover that you are not who you say you are. Can you relate to the experience of feeling anxiety in a situation that was new? That feeling was generated in response to an imagined threat, which felt real. Our primitive instinct of self-preservation frequently misjudges the level of actual danger we are in. The greater your sense of self-awareness, the more understanding you will have of how feelings surface and change.

The need to be approved of, loved and accepted will bring self-protective mechanisms into play. These conditioned reflexes prevent real connection and intimacy. Wondering what you should do in social situations suggests that you are not present. Physically, your body is there but you are so busy working things out in your head that the heart connection is blocked.

Would you like to release the energy that is blocked by fear and anxiety? If your answer is 'yes', there will be gains and losses. When you engage in ways that reflect your authentic self, you lose any fear of what others may think of you. We have already seen how attempting to put words on emotional states is a fool's errand. I suggest you would become more spontaneous and freer in yourself. You would enjoy equanimity.

Buddhists speak of equanimity, which refers to a state of mental balance, experiencing emotional calm and composure. For me, equanimity suggests that you live life on an even keel. You no longer experience the highs and lows, the blissful positive feelings when things go your way, the painful negative feelings when they don't.

When clients really engage with their personal work, they learn to slow down and see the world in a new way. I coach people to drop the sense of positive and negative feelings. What happens in you if you tell yourself, 'Even though I don't like it, it's okay'?

Accepting the things you cannot change is life-changing. 'This is how it is and that's okay' is the attitude of someone who has learned to accept life as it is and not as they want it to be. I use the coaching terminology of developing one's sense of self-understanding, self-awareness or self-care. My goal is to empower people to live spontaneously.

Words have the power to gain co-operation or to build

resistance. Clients tend to react more positively to the word 'reflection' than to the word 'introspection'. Introspection seems to bring up the fear that feelings of discomfort, pain and regret will be revealed.

If you are aware of this tendency in you, don't judge yourself. Understand that there is a subtle level of fear in you that blocks your freedom to be authentically who you are. A feeling is triggered by a thought which arises and passes away. Feelings arise and pass away.

Knowing yourself involves awareness of the mind/heart connection and the acceptance that you are responsible for your own happiness, for feelings loved and lovable. What you are aware of, you control. What you are not aware of controls you.

15

SPIRITUALITY

The amount of happiness you have in your life depends on the amount of freedom you have in your heart.

THICH NHAT HANH

I invite you to think of spirituality as a new way of looking. It transforms what you see and feel and think. It shows up flawed beliefs. People believe they see through their eyes. They don't. You cannot see anything in the absence of light.

The pupil of the eye acts like a camera aperture opening or closing to admit more or less light. The eyes autofocus as we look at nearby and distant objects. When light falls on the retina at the back of the eye, it is transmitted as electrical impulses to the optic nerve and from there to the brain. The image on the retina, which is upside down, is processed into a right-side-up image by the brain.

Can you believe what you see? If you look in a mirror, what you see is a reversed image. Put a glove on your right hand and extend your arm toward a mirror. Your reflection will appear to be wearing the glove on its left hand. The glove hasn't been altered in any way. The reflected image in the mirror is sending back exactly what you presented to it.

We are told that beauty is in the eye of the beholder. Imagine I'm looking at a beautiful sunset and someone comes up to me and asks, 'What are you looking at? You look ecstatic.' I reply, 'I'm ecstatic over the beauty. The scenery here is amazing.' The person asks, 'Where is the beauty? I only see the sun, the clouds, and the hills.'

The quality of your life is affected by what you believe to be true. Why would you allow people, places, events and thoughts to frustrate or annoy you? You would have no need to suppress negative feelings if you understand how frequently you create problems for yourself.

In the beginning, many clients resist the idea that they are giving themselves problems. Some clients are uncomfortable with the idea of the words 'spirituality' and 'religion'. No one ever objected to working with the concept that spirituality is a way of looking that transforms what you see and feel and think.

To be transformed, one must be open to see transformation. At the start, it takes an effort to learn to accept what is in front of you. What is happening inside of you determines the quality of your life. Someone criticises you, your mind generates an emotion and you feel hurt. What if you said, 'I will not let their words take my happiness away'?

Things happen and either you are okay with them or you're not. Feelings come up that are not comfortable for you. Don't waste your life trying to make them not happen. For most of your life, you numbed yourself to painful feelings. To avoid feeling uncomfortable, you unconsciously devoted yourself to controlling and manipulating the people and the things around you.

You put so much energy into attempting to have things the way you wanted them to be that you lost the ability to be fully present, to be aware of where you are and what you're doing. If you want to feel okay, develop the practice of observing your thoughts and emotions. Notice how you can let go of unwanted feelings.

You may be surprised at how easy it is to build the habit of not reacting to thoughts and emotions. You could focus on your breath when you feel a sense of discomfort. Or build the habit of saying, 'This is how it is and that is okay.'

Watch what your mind does as if it was happening to someone else. It's as if you are outside yourself watching what is happening in you. Be aware of how a fresh thought brings a new emotional response.

At a logical level, you know that you don't gain anything by upsetting yourself. In theory, you know that it is you who is in control of what you are thinking. Your programming does not control you. If you feel yourself starting to get upset, you know you can relax, breathe, and refuse to engage. Your challenge is to do this all of the time.

Transformation, spiritual growth happens when you are not pulled into thoughts and emotions. How would your life be if you had the ability to drop the concept of positive and negative emotion?

- What if you were able to allow yourself to be at ease with all emotions?
- What if you could learn to accept whatever happens in your life with no judgement or approval?
- What if you could really mean it when you say, 'This is how it is and that's okay'?

An event that used to generate stress in you would be transformed almost effortlessly. Let's imagine you are driving. The driver ahead of you is going slower than the speed limit. You feel the discomfort come up in you. Even though you don't like the feeling, you make no effort to suppress or ignore it. If you allow yourself to feel the emotion, it will surface and go. It's that simple.

There are real problems and self-generated problems in the

world. Any issue you have with the driver in front of you, who is slowing you down, is a self-generated one. Say there is a forest fire and your house is under threat. That is a real problem. You need to spring into action immediately and do something to stop it burning to the ground.

Are the problems you have with other people real or self-generated? How do you react when I suggest that how you feel about others runs your life, and affects how you react or respond? You try to control and manipulate events because you want to feel a certain way. Stop doing this to yourself.

Transformation and change come through seeing, through looking at what is happening in you with a fresh mindset. Have you issues with your partner or friend? Are you disappointed or dissatisfied? Are you sometimes depressed and anxious? People will tell you, 'That's life. It's normal and natural to experience such feelings.' Don't believe them. Your upset comes from how you choose to react.

- Think of someone you dislike.
- Pick a person you would generally avoid.
- Imagine yourself in this person's presence now.
- Watch the negative feelings come up in you.
- Ask yourself, am I in charge of this situation or is this situation in charge of me?

Understand that your negative feelings are caused not by the person, as you mistakenly believe, but by something in how you look at and see the person. What you dislike in the person may reflect something in you. Look on what you dislike as an invitation for personal growth. If your perception of a person is distorted, your thinking is wrong and your beliefs are flawed, would you want to know?

The conditioned reflex to react negatively is looked on as normal, as simply a part of life. If you blame the driver who is going too fast or too slow for upsetting you, there is something wrong with you. Your upset feelings have nothing to do with the driver, they have everything to do with what is happening in you.

Our programmed brains have a set of demands about how the world should be, how we should be and what we should want. When life fails to live up to our programmed expectations, we experience disappointment, frustration or self-blame.

Let's say you are driving mindfully and another driver beeps at you. A negative feeling is coming up in you, but it's so strong that you can't let it go. Don't feel stressed or judge yourself. Look on this as a good thing. Isn't it beautiful that you're aware of what is happening inside of you? It tells you, you have more work to do. Think of it as an opportunity to engage more with the work of letting go.

Never blame anyone for upsetting your feelings. Feelings are transitory. They arise and pass away. When you look from a spiritual perspective, you will see that your fears and your negative feelings have nothing to do with the circumstances of life but the effect life has on you.

When I was about ten years of age, I found the courage to ask a nun how a loving God could put people in hell. I was told I asked too many questions, and warned that questioning my faith was a sign of pride, and pride was one of the seven deadly sins. She warned me that I was on the slippery slope to hell. The fear of burning in the agony of hell fires, punished for all eternity because I displeased God perplexed me, especially as a sinner could go to confession to be cleansed from their sins.

Catholic Christians have the sacrament of confession, which

Spirituality

for the uninitiated can be described as a 'get out of hell card'. There is a lovely story told about the young boy who wanted a bicycle. His priest told him to have faith that no prayer goes unanswered. So, he prayed and he prayed and he prayed. Weeks went by and months went by and no bicycle. Then one day, the priest saw him riding a brand new bicycle. 'What a blessing that God has answered your prayer,' the priest said. 'No,' said the boy. 'I got tired of praying so I stole the bicycle but don't worry, Father. I've been to confession and God has forgiven me.'

Early on your spiritual journey, it will take an effort to be open, to let feelings surface and go. Stay neutral, don't analyse or blame. If you do this constantly, you will begin to see how your ability to love can be diminished if your heart is hardened by emotional pain. In the measure that you numb yourself to emotional pain, you lose the capacity to love.

A hardened heart is akin to a callus that builds up to protect sensitive areas of the body. Thickening skin is the body's protective method to cushion physical discomfort. Shutting down emotional pain is a protective measure. Numbing yourself to unwanted feelings may shield you from pain, but it will also desensitise you to positive emotions.

The daily practice of meditation will bring you to see this and will soften the heart. You will begin to identify the programmed reactions to events you do not control. As you become more practised at self-observation, there will be times when you find yourself watching yourself and wincing. Don't bother asking, 'How did I allow myself to get so upset?' Decide, 'I will not do this to myself anymore.' If you create a problem inside yourself, you need to resolve the problem.

Frustration, fear and disappointment will come up in you and when they come up, don't resist. Learn to let your feelings surface and go. As you do this, little by little you will develop the awareness to notice the shift when you begin to feel disturbed. If you feel frustrated, fear or anger, it's simply because you feel frustrated, fear and anger.

Watch for what makes you feel better inside or worse inside. When you experience emotional pain, can you sit there without getting sucked in to a programmed response? There are two emotions: love and fear. If fear comes up in you, can you be conscious of observing the fear? In the absence of fear, you will experience the freedom to love with all of your heart and mind and spirit.

If you want to love, you must learn to look and see with new eyes. With practice, you can learn to observe yourself wishing you didn't feel fear and allow yourself to keep watching. When you make the effort to remain present, what will happen is you will hone your ability to remain calm, peaceful and aware even when you don't like whatever feelings you experience.

There is only one reason why you are not blissfully happy. It's that you're not aware of the programmed beliefs that control your thinking. Understand your wrong or flawed beliefs. Drop them and you will be filled with compassion and have the freedom to experience love without fear.

If you look externally for your needs and desires to be met, you distract yourself from what is happening internally in you. You were programmed to believe that it is natural to feel upset if your partner fails to fulfil a promise. Did anyone explain that what was really going on is that you wanted something that you didn't get? You were conditioned to believe that it was normal to react with disappointed and hurt feelings.

If your goal is to feel happy, fulfilled and excited about your life, it helps to develop a new way of looking. When a partner is seen through rose-tinted spectacles, it is easy to be blind to character traits that may disappoint, frustrate and irritate when reality sets in. I once had a client who asked herself the question, 'What am I doing with this person?' on her honeymoon.

The positive intention of people who suppress their feelings is to avoid feeling uncomfortable. Do you understand that everything you experience is connected to your thoughts and emotions? Your heart and mind are connected. If you think it is easier to ignore or deny emotional pain than to face reality, you are blind to reality. If you feel frustrated, angry or upset with your partner, your reaction is generated by thoughts in your mind.

Thoughts that come from your programmed thinking block the body, mind and heart connection. To believe that many of their negative feelings are caused by self-generated problems is too much of a challenge for some clients. It's all very well to give credence to the theory that each of us is responsible for our own happiness. To put the theory into practice is a daily challenge.

Letting go of the wrong beliefs and conditioned reflexes that contribute to emotional pain and distress is an essential part of the quest for happiness. You were brainwashed into believing that to be happy you needed to become successful, have a career, money, a loving partner and all the trappings of worldly success.

Could you be happy with none of these? Are you aware of your reaction as you read these words? Are you simultaneously aware of where your reaction came from? Did it come from your programming or from you?

You will not be able to change your programming quickly and you may not need to. If you wish to be happy, the first thing you need is to have a clear understanding of how you have been programmed. All you need to do is open your eyes and pay close attention to what is happening in you and around you.

Anthony de Mello, SJ, one of the most gifted spiritual teachers of the twentieth century, described self-awareness as the 'I' watching 'me'. Self-observation means watching what is going on in you and around you as if it were happening to someone else. You observe yourself feeling happy. Who or what is the 'you' that is aware of your happiness? If you hold out your hand, 'Who is seeing the hand you are holding out?'

Becoming aware of how positive and negative feelings arise in 'me' takes daily practice and self-awareness. If your partner tells you, 'You're a wonderful person', who is your partner talking about? Words such as you're wonderful, successful, wealthy, or famous only apply to 'me'. They are labels for states that very easily can be taken from you.

You may think of the good feelings caused by external events such as the status job, the big house, the fast car as happiness. It's a 'happiness' that can go if the job is lost or the house burns down or the car is replaced by a newer, faster model. The quality of the interior experience when a baby smiles and your heart softens in response is different; as is the heartfelt response to an act of kindness.

I have never worked with a genuinely spiritual person who was anti-religion. I've worked with numerous religious people who were anything but spiritual. I'm a nature lover. When I look at a beautiful sunset, I feel a sense of awe and reverence and I am filled with gratitude for a God-given sense of the divine. I love that the *Oxford Dictionary* gives two meanings for the word 'divine'. One is, 'of or like God or a god'. The other is 'very pleasing; delightful'.

SPIRITUALITY

There is a lovely story to explain how religion got God a bad name, because of what was said of him from pulpits. I went with my friend to the World Fair of Religions. The competition was fierce, the propaganda loud. At the Jewish stall, we were given handouts that said God was all compassionate and the Jews were his chosen people. The Jews said no other people were as chosen as they were. At the Muslim stall, we learned that God was all merciful and Muhammed is his only prophet. Salvation comes from listening to God's prophet.

At the Christian stall, we discovered that God is love and there is no salvation outside the Church. Join the Church or risk eternal damnation. On the way out, I asked my friend, 'What do you think of God?' 'He is bigoted, fanatical and cruel' was her reply. Back home, I said to God, 'How do you put up with this sort of thing, Lord? Don't you see they have been giving you a bad name for centuries?' God said, 'It wasn't I who organised the fair. In fact, I'd be too ashamed to visit it.'

Both good and evil have been done in the name of religion. Church leaders preach that God is love and tell us that we are to love our neighbours as ourselves. If they practised what they preached, would there have been 'holy wars', Muslims fighting against Jews, Catholic Christians against Protestants and Buddhists against Hindus?

The two words 'spirituality' and 'religion' are often used interchangeably. In a coaching context, the word 'spirituality' may never be mentioned. To excel and reach their full potential, I encourage each client to focus on knowing yourself, and knowing who you are. A coach who has a holistic approach will not need to renegotiate the coaching contract when a client's religious beliefs are an integral part of their spiritual journey. The words 'mindfulness' and 'meditation' are used interchangeably. I look on mindfulness as self-awareness, learning to relax through sitting quietly to calm the mind and destress.

When writing about spirituality and religion, it is incredibly difficult to find the language to communicate clearly and without causing offence to someone who has a negative reaction to either word. 'Religion' has been defined as the belief in and worship of a superhuman power or powers, especially a God or gods. My favourite definition of 'spirituality' is, 'Spirituality means never to be upset by any person, place, event or thing. Religion is meant to lead to spirituality, frequently it doesn't.'

Religious people use words such as worship, prayer, meditation or contemplation to describe their spiritual practices. A recognised practice in countless religions is spiritual meditation. Its purpose is to silence thought, clear the mind and deepen the connection to God, a higher power, the divine, or to someone or something that is greater than oneself.

When the dressmaker Mademoiselle Rose Bertin refashioned a dress for French queen Marie Antoinette, she is reported to have said, 'There is nothing new except what has been forgotten.' It's not my intention to be disrespectful when I suggest that teachings about prayer, spiritual meditation and mindfulness are constantly refashioned.

Numerous renowned teachers offer techniques for helping meditators to sit quietly, still the mind and practise being in the present moment. Professor Emeritus Jon Kabat-Zinn, founder and former director of the Stress Reduction Clinic at the University of Massachusetts, brought the practice of mindfulness to the general public as if it was something new and innovative rather than a form of meditation dating back thousands of years.

In the 1960s and 1970s, Herbert Benson was a pioneer in mind/body medicine. He worked to build awareness of it, to validate it through research and to bridge the gap between Eastern and Western medical practices. Director Emeritus of the Benson-Henry Institute and Mind Body Professor of Medicine at Harvard Medical School, Benson was one of the first Western physicians to bring spirituality and healing into medicine.

He conducted studies that showed that people who meditate regularly enjoyed lower stress levels, had increased wellbeing and some were able to reduce their blood pressure levels and resting heart rate. His book on meditation, which he called *The Relaxation Response*, became an instant bestseller and motivated millions of people worldwide to practise meditation. Some of the better-known teachers of meditation as a form of prayer are Benedictine monk John Main, Trappist monk Thomas Keating and Carthusian Monk, Thomas Merton.

The form of Christian meditation taught by John Main focused on breath concentration or the repetition of a mantra. He said, 'The all-important aim in Christian meditation is to allow God's mysterious and silent presence within us to become more and more not only a reality, but the reality which gives meaning, shape and purpose to everything we do, to everything we are.'

He taught people to 'Sit down. Sit still and upright. Close your eyes lightly. Sit relaxed but alert. Silently, interiorly begin to say a single word.' He recommended the prayer-phrase 'Maranatha' to be recited as four syllables of equal length. His suggestion was that you listen to it as you say it, gently but continuously. You are not to think or imagine anything spiritual or otherwise. If thoughts or images come, these are distractions at the time of meditation, so you keep returning to simply saying the word. He believed that one result of this prayer is that it gives reality, meaning, shape, and purpose to everything we do, to everything we are.

Trappist monk Thomas Keating made centring prayer popular. He had a spiritual experience and realised that union with the divine is not only possible but available to all. He defined centring prayer as 'a very simple method in which one opens one's self to God and consents to his presence in us and to his actions within us.' Beyond words, emotions, and thoughts, centring prayer, Keating said, is like 'two friends sitting in silence, just being in each other's presence'.

Physicians, academics, monks and priests encourage the practice of meditation because it meets a human need. Through the centuries, millions of people worldwide engaged in these practices because of the benefits they gained. The daily practice of seeking interior silence gives peace of mind.

Teachers of mindfulness, meditation and prayer have a common purpose, the silencing of the thoughts churning in the mind that generate stress. Some people look for techniques that will help them shift their thoughts away from their usual preoccupations. In my experience, clients who have a daily practice don't necessarily benefit from techniques.

In the book *Wellsprings*, Anthony de Mello, SJ has a beautiful meditation in which he says:

- There is no need for any thought or sentiments or any special insights.
- Only be aware of the hearing activity of the self,
- Or the breathing activity of the self.
- And you will come home, back to yourself and the self will become silent.
- And God will not be far away.

Spirituality is for people of all religions and people of none.

Readers who have an issue with the word God might like to substitute, 'And love that opens the heart will not be far away' for the last line of the meditation.

Psychologist and Jesuit priest Anthony de Mello taught that there were four stages in prayer:

- I talk God listens.
- God talks I listen.
- Neither talks, both listen.
- Silence.

Religious faith gifts you with the spiritual eyes to see yourself, your life, everyone and everything in the world as a gift from God. When you take a breath, when you walk, when you talk, you are experiencing a divine gift. Seeing the spiritual presence in all things, you cannot know yourself apart from God. This knowing takes you beyond words and thoughts, to become fearless and free to be Who You Are.

At the start of this chapter, I invited you to think of spirituality as a new way of looking, which transforms what you see and feel and think. Can you imagine how blissful, happy, and fulfilled you would feel if you had no fear that something could go wrong? Some feelings come up in you as you read this. Can you be okay with them?

Learn to be okay with every feeling because no feeling is good or bad, it simply is. What were you looking for when you set out on a quest for happiness? Happiness is an experience that cannot be described.

I've named many of the beliefs that are an obstacle to happiness. I've explained how you can train yourself to feel all your emotions. When you are willing to sit with uncomfortable feelings, you will discover that you can calmly handle events that once were stressful. You will develop a sense of compassion and tolerance for yourself when old patterns of behaviour emerge.

If you are intolerant with yourself, your focus is on what you don't want. This makes it more likely that unwanted behaviour will reoccur. You will still feel annoyed, indignant or angry but the tendency to judge yourself will wane. You will simply be a neutral observer.

The highs and lows of the past will no longer affect you. At face value, nothing much will have changed. Internally, you will be free because you are in a state when you refuse to allow any person, place, event or thing to generate upset in you.

Some people say that spiritual transformation occurs through a source that is deep within them. Others believe it occurs through their own efforts and hard work. People of faith believe it happens by the divine grace of God, their higher power or a spiritual source.

Lao Tzu said of spiritually awakened people, 'Those who know do not speak. Those who speak do not know.'

Epilogue

Though nobody can go back and make a new beginning, anyone can start over and make a new ending.

Chico Xavier

Your thoughts, words and actions determine the quality of your happiness and will affect all of your relationships. In theory, how happy you feel is largely determined by you, by how you respond and react to what you think. In practice, most people do not believe that they control their thoughts.

The theory is that we can speedily dismiss the random thoughts that pop into our minds. That is not my, and probably not your, experience. To ignore and forget about thoughts is easier said than done.

We are told that people are more likely to be at their happiest when they are living in line with their values. People's values change over time. Values that were important to you as a single person can change when you are living with a partner or have a child. Our lives would be so different if from infancy we were taught to love and accept ourselves exactly as we are and not as others would like us to be.

Couple relationships would be emotionally healthier if we were never exposed to the 'happy ever after' myth. When the romantic myth is shattered and partners have realistic expectations of what an emotionally healthy partnership is like, they become liberated and free to be themselves.

For over twenty years, I coached couples who wanted better relationships. They were staying together because they were not financially able to divorce or for the sake of their children. When partners are no longer having sex, when intimacy is gone and most conversations are about practical matters, a partnership is in trouble.

A big step in healing any relationship is to learn how miscommunication breeds misunderstanding. Coaching partners and individuals to explore how their beliefs and values affected their thoughts and actions was life-changing. A client who recognised that their partner did not make them happy learned an important life lesson: You can be happy with and without a partner.

Working through the exercises in this book may be like holding a mirror up to see a reflection of how your beliefs and expectations may be blocking your happiness. There are no perfect lives, no perfect partnerships, and no perfect families.

In a coaching context, clients explore how their beliefs affect their outlook in life. As the practice of meditation became more popular, I found that many clients became deeply reflective. They explored questions such as, 'Who am I?' 'What am I here for?' and 'What is my place in the world?'.

A small number experienced a deep sense of being connected to something larger or greater than the self. They felt connected to a source that gave them strength, and their lives a deeper meaning. Some felt supported, others felt calmer and more peaceful. I think of these as spiritual experiences that allow a person's inner radiance to emerge and shine.

I love the sentiments in Marianne Williamson's poem, 'Our Deepest Fear'. My hope for you is that you will come to recognise that you are powerful beyond measure, that you are brilliant, gorgeous, talented and fabulous. My prayer for you is that you will come to love who you are, connect with the radiance of your own spirit, and let your light shine.

BIBLIOGRAPHY

Alder, Harry and Heather, Beryl, *NLP in 12 Days* (Piatkus, London, 1999)
Allen, Roger P., *Scripts and Strategies in Hypnotherapy, Vol 1* (Crown House Publishing, Carmarthen, 1997)
Amen, Daniel G. MD, *Change Your Brain, Change Your Life* (Little Brown Book Group, New York, 1998)
Andreas, Connirae, PhD and Andreas, Steve, MA, *Heart of the Mind: Engaging your Inner Power to Change with Neuro Linguistic Programming* (Real People Press, Moab, Utah, USA 1989)
—— *Change your Mind – And Keep the Change* (Real People Press, Moab, Utah, USA, 1987)
Andreas, Connirae and Andreas, Tamara, *Core Transformation: Reaching the Wellspring Within* (Real People Press, Moab, Utah, USA, 1994)
Andreas, Steve and Faulkner, Charles, *NLP: The New Technology of Achievement* (Nicholas Brealey Publishing, London, 1996)
Bandler, Richard, *Using Your Brain for a CHANGE* (Real People Press, Moab, Utah, USA, 1985)
Bandler, Richard and Grinder, John, *Frogs into Princes: Neuro Linguistic Programming* (Real People Press, Moab, Utah, 1979)
—— *The Structure of Magic I* (Science and Behavior Books, Palo Alto, CA, USA, 1975)
—— *The Structure of Magic II* (Science and Behavior Books, Palo Alto, CA, USA, 1989)
Bandler, Richard and MacDonald, Will, *An Insider's Guide to Sub-Modalities* (Meta Publications, Capitola, CA, USA, 1988)
Battino, Rubin and South, Thomas L., *Ericksonian Approaches* (Crown House Publishing, Carmarthen, 1999)
Best, Ron, Lang, Peter, Lodge, Caroline, and Watkins, Chris, *Pastoral Care and Personal-Social Education* (Cassell, London, 1995)
Bloom, Allan, *Love and Friendship* (Simon & Schuster, New York, USA, 1993)
Bodenhamer, Bob G. and Hall, L. Michael, *The User's Manual for the Brain* (Crown House Publishing, Carmarthen, 1999)
Bradbury, Andrew, *Develop Your NLP Skills* (Kogan Page, London, 2000)
Bradshaw, John, *Family Secrets* (Bantam, USA, 1995)
—— *Homecoming* (Piatkus, Houston, USA, 1990)
—— *The Family* (HCI, Florida, USA, 1988)

—— *Healing the Shame that Binds You* (HCI, Florida, USA, 1988)
Cameron-Bandler, Leslie, *Solutions: Enhancing Love, Sex and Relationships* (Real People Press, Moab, Utah, USA, 1985)
Cameron-Bandler, Leslie and Lebeau, Michael, *The Emotional Hostage* (People Press, Moab, Utah, USA, 1986)
Canfield, Jack, *How to Get from Where You Are to Where You Want to Be* (Harper Collins, Element, UK, 2007)
Chapman, Gary, *The Five Love Languages* (Northfield Publishing, USA, 1992)
Chopra, Deepak, *Unconditional Life* (Bantam Books, New York, 1991)
Corey, Gerald, *Theory and Practice of Counselling and Psychotherapy*, 6th Edition (Wadsworth, London, 2001)
Culley, Sue, *Integrative Counselling Skills in Action* (Sage Publications, London, 1991)
Davis Brigham, Deirdre, *Imagery for Getting Well* (W.W. Norton & Co, New York, USA, 1996)
De Mello, Anthony, SJ, *Walking on Water* (Columba Press, Dublin, 1992)
—— *Wellsprings* (Gujarat Sahitya Prakash, Anand, India, 1992)
DeLozier, Judith and Grinder, John, *Turtles All the Way Down* (Grinder, DeLozier & Associates, California, USA, 1987)
Egan, Gerard, *The Skilled Helper* (7th Edition) (Brooks/Cole, Pacific Grove, California, USA, 2001)
Fisher, Helen, *Why Him? Why Her?* (Henry Holt & Co, USA, 2009)
Foreman, Elaine Iljon and Pollard, Clair, *Cognitive Behavioural Therapy (CBT)* (Icon Books Limited, UK, 2016)
Gaffney, Maureen, *Flourishing* (Penguin Ireland, 2011)
Gibb, Barry J., *The Rough Guide To The Brain* (Rough Guides Ltd, UK, 2007)
Gibran, Kahlil, *The Prophet* (Oneworld Publications, Oxford, 1995)
Goleman, Daniel, *Emotional Intelligence* (Bloomsbury, UK, 1995
Gray, John, *Men are from Mars, Women are from Venus* (Thorsons, London, 1992)
—— *How to Get What You Want and Want What You Have* (Vermilion, London, 1999)
Greenberger, Dennis PhD and Padesky, Christine A. PhD, *Mind Over Mood* (Guilford Press, New York, USA, 1995)
Haidt, Jonathan, *The Happiness Hypothesis* (Hachette Book Group Unit, USA, 2006)
Hall, L. Michael and Bodenhamer, Bob G., *Figuring Out People: Design Engineering with Meta Programs* (Crown House Publishing, Carmarthen, 1997)
—— *The User's Manual for the Brain* (Crown House Publishing,

Carmarthen, 1999)
Harris, Thomas A., *I'm OK, You're OK* (Pan Books, London, 1973)
Hornby, Albert Sydney, *Oxford Advanced Learner's Dictionary of Current English*, Jonathan Crowther (ed.) (Oxford University Press, Oxford, 1995)
Humphreys, Tony, *Myself, My Partner* (Gill & Macmillan, Dublin 1997)
Jung, Carl, *Memories, Dreams, Reflections* (Vintage, New York, 1989)
Leaf, Caroline, *Cleaning Up Your Mental Mess* (Baker Books, Ada, Michigan, USA, 2021)
—— *Switch On Your Brain* ((Baker Books, Ada, Michigan, USA, 2018)
Main, John, *The Way of Unknowing: Expanding Spiritual Horizons through meditation* (Darton, Longman & Todd, UK, 1989)
Mandel, Debbie, *Addicted to Stress* (Jossey-Bass, San Francisco, USA, 2008)
May, Rollo, *Freedom and Destiny* (Norton, USA, 2012)
McDermott, Ian and O'Connor, Joseph, *Neuro-Linguistic Programming (NLP) and Health* (Thorsons, London, 1966)
McGraw, Dr Phillip C., *Relationship Rescue* (Vermilion, London, 2000)
—— *Life Strategies* (Vermilion, London, 1999)
McHugh, Richard P., *Mind with a Heart* (Gujarat Sahitya Prakash, India, 1998)
Merton, Thomas, *New Seeds of Contemplation* (New Directions, USA, 1972)
Mulligan, Eileen, *Life Coaching: Change your life in 7 days* (Piatkus, London, 1999)
Neff, Dr Kristin, Self-Compassion, https://self-compassion.org.
Nelson-Jones, Richard, *Human Relationship Skills* (Cassell, London, 1986)
O'Connor, Joseph, *NLP Workbook* (Thorsons, London, 2001)
O'Connor, Joseph and Prior, Robin, *NLP & Relationships* (Thorsons, London, 2000)
O'Connor, Joseph and Seymour, John, *Introducing NLP* (2nd Edition) (Thorsons, London, 1995)
—— *with NLP* (Thorsons, London, 1994)
Pearsall, Judy, *The New Oxford Dictionary of English* (Oxford University Press, Oxford, 2001)
Powell, John, SJ, *The Secret of Staying in Love* (Thomas More, Allen, Texas, USA, 2017)
—— *Unconditional Love* (Thomas More, Allen, Texas, USA, 1989)
—— *Why Am I Afraid to Love?* (Thomas More, Allen, Texas, USA, 1972)
—— *Happiness is an Inside Job* (Thomas More, Allen, Texas, USA, 1989)

—— *Fully Human, Fully Alive* (Thomas More, Allen, Texas, USA, 1976)
—— *Why Am I Afraid to Tell You Who I Am?* (Thomas More, Allen, Texas, USA, 1969)
Powell, John, SJ and Brady, Loretta, *Will the Real Me Please Stand Up?* (Thomas More, Allen, Texas, USA, 1985)
Prior, Robin and O'Connor, Joseph, *NLP & Relationships* (Thorsons, London, 2000)
Richardson, Cheryl, *Life Makeovers* (Bantam Books, UK, 2001)
Robbins, Anthony, *Unlimited Power: The new Science of Personal Achievement* (Simon & Schuster, New York, 1997)
—— *Awaken the Giant Within: How to take control of your mental, emotional, physical and financial destiny* (Simon&Schuster,NewYork,USA,1992)
Robson, David, *The Expectation Effect* (Canongate Books, UK, 2022)
Rogers, Carl, *On Becoming a Person* (Constable, London, 1961)
Rosenthal, Don and Martha, *Intimacy, The Noble Adventure* (The Collins Press, Cork, 1999)
Satir, Virginia, *Peoplemaking* (Science and Behavior Books, Palo Alto, California, 1972)
—— *Making Contact* (Celestial Arts, Berkeley, California, USA, 1976)
Sheehy, Gail, *New Passages* (HarperCollins, London, UK, 1996)
Singer, Michael A., *The Untethered Soul* (New Harbinger Publications Inc, Oakland, California, USA, 2007)
Skynner, Robin and Cleese, John, *Life and How to Survive It* (Mandarin, London, 1996, ©1993)
St John of the Cross, *The Dark Night of the Soul* (Hodder & Stoughton, UK, 1979)
Stevens, John O., *Awareness: Exploring, Experimenting, Experiencing* (Eden Grove Editions, London, 1989)
Tannen, Deborah, *The Argument Culture* (Virago Press, London, 1998)
—— *I Only Say This Because I Love You* (Virago Press, London, 2001)
Tolle, Eckhart, *A New Earth* (Penguin Books, New York, USA, 2016)
Van Breemen, Peter G., SJ, *As Bread That is Broken* (Dimension Books, Denville, NJ, USA, 1974)
Vanzant, Iyanla, *In the Meantime* (Pocket Books, USA, 1999)
Wynne, Carmel, *Relationships and Sexuality* (Mercier Press, Cork, 1997)
—— *Sex and Young People: The Knowledge to Guide the Teenager in Your Life* (Mercier Press, Cork, 2001)
—— *Coaching: The Key to Unlocking Your Potential* (Beache Key Publications, Dublin, 2003)
Zagler, Zig, *See You at the Top* (Pelican Publishing Company, Gretna, Louisianna, USA, 1984)
Zukav, Gary, *The Seat of the Soul* (Simon & Schuster, New York, USA, 1989)